Strategies to Integrate the *Arts* in Social Studies

Authors

Jennifer M. Bogard, M.Ed.
Maureen Creegan-Quinquis, M.F.A, M.Ed.

LESLEY
UNIVERSITY

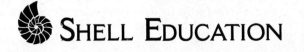

SHELL EDUCATION

Publishing Credits

Dona Herweck Rice, *Editor-in-Chief*; Robin Erickson, *Production Director*; Lee Aucoin, *Creative Director*; Timothy J. Bradley, *Illustration Manager*; Sara Johnson, M.S.Ed., *Editorial Director*; Tracy Edmunds, *Editor*; Leah Quillian, *Assistant Editor*; Grace Alba, *Designer*; Corinne Burton, *M.A.Ed., Publisher*

Series Editors

Lisa Donovan, Ph.D., Associate Professor, Massachusetts College of Liberal Arts, Fine and Performing Arts

Linda Dacey, Ed.D., Professor of Education and Mathematics, Lesley University

Collaborating Author

Jonathan Wheeler, M.Ed., Social Studies Teacher, Auburn Village School, Auburn, NH

Contributing Authors

Louise Pascale, Ph.D., Associate Professor, Lesley University Creative Arts in Learning Division

Celeste Miller, Adjunct Faculty, Lesley University Creative Arts in Learning Division

David Williams, M.Ed., Grade 4 Teacher, Newbury Elementary School, MA

Brittany Williams, M.Ed., Grade 3 Teacher, Newbury Elementary School, MA

Tanya West, Music Teacher, Theater Manager and Director, MSAD 35

Consultants

Mary Ann Cappiello, Ed.D., Associate Professor of Language and Literacy, Lesley University

Rebecca E. Woodman, M.Ed., Speech and Language Pathologist, Central Elementary School, South Berwick, ME

Che' Madyun, Senior Adjunct Professor, Cambridge College, Community Arts, Dance, Theater

Sarah Gurley-Green, M.A., Doctoral Candidate Lesley University, www.gurleygreen.com

Elyse H. Rast, Doctoral Candidate, M.S. Elementary Education, B.S. Speech Communication, B.S. Communications Studies, Holocaust and Genocide Educator

Ann Mechem Ziergiebel, M.Ed., Adolescent Education and Leadership, Salem State University, Doctoral Candidate Lesley University

Principal Vicki Stewart, M.Ed., MSAD 35

Principal Nina D'Aran, B.S. Elementary Education, M.A. Counseling Psychology, Doctoral Candidate Educational Leadership, Central School, South Berwick, ME

Grace S. Jacobs, M.Ed., MSAD 35

Image Credits

p. 198 LOC [LC-USZ62-69643]; p. 199 LOC [LC-USF34-043862-D]; p. 200 [LC-DIG-ppmsca-25745]; all other images Shutterstock

Standards

© 2004 Mid-continent Research for Education and Learning (McREL)
© 2007 Teachers of English to Speakers of Other Languages, Inc. (TESOL)
© 2007 Board of Regents of the University of Wisconsin System. World-Class Instructional Design and Assessment (WIDA). For more information on using the WIDA ELP Standards, please visit the WIDA website at www.wida.us.
© 2010 National Governors Association Center for Best Practices and Council of Chief State School Officers (CCSS)

Shell Education

5301 Oceanus Drive
Huntington Beach, CA 92649-1030
http://www.shelleducation.com

ISBN 978-1-4258-1092-4

© 2013 Shell Educational Publishing, Inc.

Table of Contents

The Importance of Arts Integration

Teachers have an important and challenging job, and it seems that they are asked to do more with each passing year. Lesley University professors in the Creative Arts Division hear from teachers regularly that integrating the arts would be a great thing to do if they just had time and support. Yet research shows that integration of the arts is an efficient and effective strategy for addressing some of the greatest challenges in today's educational landscape as the arts deepen learning in ways that engage all learners of all abilities and needs (President's Committee on the Arts and the Humanities 2011; Burnaford 2007). Study after study points to compelling evidence of the significant outcomes that are linked to arts integration.

According to the President's Committee on the Arts and the Humanities, "studies have now documented significant links between arts integration models and academic and social outcomes for students, efficacy for teachers, and school-wide improvements in culture and climate. Arts integration is efficient, addressing a number of outcomes at the same time. Most important, the greatest gains in schools with arts integration are often seen school-wide and also with the most hard-to-reach and economically disadvantaged students" (2011).

A recent study, funded by the Ford Foundation and led by researchers from Lesley University's Creative Arts in Learning Division and an external advisory team, conducted research with more than 200 Lesley alumni teaching across the country who had been trained in arts-integration strategies. The findings suggest that arts-integrated teaching provides a variety of strategies for accessing content and expressing understanding of learning that is culturally responsive and relevant in students' lives. This leads to deep learning, increased student ownership, and engagement with academic content. Not only does arts integration engage students in creativity, innovation, and imagination, but also it renews teachers' commitment to teaching (Bellisario and Donovan with Prendergast 2012).

Really, then, the question becomes this: *How can we afford not to provide students with access to the arts as an engaging way to learn and express ideas across the curriculum?*

Arts integration is the investigation of curricular content through artistic explorations where the arts provide an avenue for rigorous investigation, representation, expression, and reflection of both curricular content and the art form itself (Diaz, Donovan, and Pascale 2006). This book provides teachers with concrete strategies to integrate the arts across the curriculum. Arts-integration strategies are introduced with contextual information about the art form (creative movement, drama, music, poetry, storytelling, and visual arts).

The Importance of Arts Integration *(cont.)*

Each art form provides you with new ways to help students fully engage with content and participate in memorable learning experiences. Creative movement allows students to embody ideas and work conceptually. Drama challenges students to explore multiple perspectives of characters, historical figures, and scientists. Music develops students' ability to listen, to generate a sense of community, and to communicate and connect aurally. Poetry invites students to build a more playful, fresh relationship with written and spoken language. Storytelling connects students with roots in the oral tradition and heightens their awareness of the role stories play in their lives. Visual art taps into students' ability to observe critically, envision, think through metaphor, and build visual literacy in a world where images are pervasive.

Providing learners with the opportunity to investigate concepts and express their understanding with the powerful languages of the arts will deepen students' understanding, heighten their curiosity, and bring forward their voices as they interact more fully with content and translate their ideas into new forms. This book is a beginning, a "way in."

We invite you to see for yourself by bringing the strategies shared in this book to your classroom and seeing what happens. We hope this resource leaves you looking for deeper experiences with the arts both for you and for your students.

What Does It Mean to Integrate the Arts?

As stated by the National Council for the Social Studies in its revised curriculum standards, "the primary purpose of social studies is to help young people make informed and reasoned decisions for the public good as citizens of a culturally diverse, democratic society in an interdependent world" (1994, 3). Yet social studies is often taught in ways that leave students unengaged and wondering, "What does this have to do with me?" (Rosler 2008). When teachers emphasize rote learning over conceptual development or quick, broad coverage of content over deep understanding, it is no wonder that many students rate social studies as one of their least-liked subjects in school. However, social studies is meaningful when students are taught multiple perspectives and learn through the lens of untold stories of people in different circumstances and in different times. Social studies supports the development of critical thinking skills and civic responsibility.

Most of us recognize that there are many connections between the arts and social studies. After all, the arts are both a product of and a window into particular places and times. Teachers may teach works of art that depict a particular historical period or songs that communicate the struggles, desires, and hopes of people of the past and present. Integrating the arts and social studies can promote student understanding of "the meaning and importance of historical events; patterns that have occurred over time and implications for today's world; and the significance of historical events on people's lives and the shared experiences of people over time and across cultures" (Miller et al. 1989).

The Importance of Arts Integration (*cont.*)

What we are aiming for here, though, is a seamless blending of the two areas in a sustained manner. We will guide you in the use of the arts and provide a context in which social studies concepts take shape and deepen while the arts inform and enrich the lives of your students. We do not want you to do this in a tangential manner or just on an enrichment basis. Rather, we want you to use arts integration as an approach to teaching the most prevalent standards in your social studies curriculum and to do so frequently. By teaching social studies ideas through artistic explorations, you will help your students develop skills and knowledge in both disciplines. We will share strategies with you that are flexible enough to be used across content strands and grade levels.

Why Should I Integrate the Arts?

Instruction in English language arts and mathematics continues to dominate classroom instruction and mandated assessments. Government-led initiatives such as No Child Left Behind focus on these two subjects. With the release of the Common Core State Standards (National Governors Association Center for Best Practices and Council of Chief State School Officers 2012) for English Language Arts and Mathematics, even more focus has shifted to these two areas. Yet as educators, we want to teach the whole child. Students need both the arts and social studies to live in and make sense of today's diverse and complex world.

The revised position statement of the National Council for the Social Studies states that "education for citizenship has taken a back seat to education for career and college" (2008). Laurel Schmidt warns us that "results from the most recent national civics exam showed that fewer than half of American eighth graders knew the purpose of the Bill of Rights and three-quarters of high school seniors were unable to name a power granted to Congress by the Constitution" (2011, 47). Clearly, we need to make time in our curriculum to teach these important concepts.

The Common Core State Standards give significant attention to using English language arts to understand other subject areas. This emphasis provides educators with the opportunity to give more attention to social studies. The Common Core State Standards also encourage students to consult primary sources that are the "raw materials of history—original documents and objects which were created at the time under study" ("Using Primary Sources" 2013). Learning about social studies through the arts is a natural bridge to the past.

Research suggests that academic achievement may be linked to the arts (Kennedy 2006). As noted by Douglas Reeves, "the challenge for school leaders is to offer every student a rich experience with the arts without sacrificing the academic opportunities students need" (2007, 80). By integrating the arts with social studies, we are able to highlight social studies ideas within rich settings and provide our students with access to the arts. In fact, the arts can lead to "deep learning" where students are more genuinely engaged with academic content, spend more time on task, and take ownership of their learning (Bellisario and Donovan with Prendergast 2012).

The Importance of Arts Integration *(cont.)*

Rinne et al. (2011) identify several ways in which arts integration improves long-term retention through elaboration, enactment, and rehearsal. Specifically, when learners create and add details to their own visual models, dramatize a concept or skill, sing a song repeatedly, or rehearse for a performance, they are increasing the likelihood that they will remember what they have learned. This retention lasts not just for the next chapter test but over significant periods of time. Through repetition that doesn't feel like "drill and kill," this information is retained for life because students become deeply engaged when working in arts integration. They eagerly revisit, review, rehearse, edit, and work through ideas repeatedly and in authentic ways as they translate ideas into new forms.

As brain research deepens our understanding of how learning takes place, educators have come to better appreciate the importance of the arts. The arts support communication, emotional connections, community, and higher-order thinking. They are also linked to increased academic achievement, especially among at-risk students. Eric Jensen argues that the "arts enhance the process of learning. The systems they nourish, which include our integrated sensory, attentional, cognitive, emotional, and motor capabilities, are, in fact, the driving forces behind all other learning" (2001, 2). Lessons and activities that integrate social studies and the arts provide a rich environment for the exploration of social studies content for all students and particularly for those students who need new ways to access curriculum and express understanding as well as providing another source of motivation.

The Center for Applied Special Technology (2012) suggests that in meeting the needs of variable learners, educators should expand their teaching to provide universal design. That is, that teachers include strategies that "are flexible and responsive to the needs of all learners" by providing "multiple means of engagement, methods of presentation of content, and multiple avenues for expression of understanding." The integration of the arts provides opportunities to address universal design principles.

Arts and the Standards

Essential Qualities of a Social Studies Program

In its position paper, the National Council for the Social Studies (2008) states that social studies teaching and learning are powerful when they are:

1. Meaningful
2. Integrative
3. Value-based
4. Challenging
5. Active

We believe that integration with the arts will increase the likelihood of social studies lessons matching these descriptors. The lessons in this book were developed with these goals in mind.

Artistic Habits of Mind

As well as essential qualities of social studies programs, students will also be developing artistic habits of mind (Hetland et al. 2007). With these habits of mind, students will become able to:

1. Develop craft
2. Engage and persist
3. Envision
4. Express
5. Observe
6. Reflect
7. Stretch and explore
8. Understand the art world

Though these habits were identified in an investigation of visual-art practices, they are relevant for the practice of all of the arts. As students engage in social studies lessons through these lenses, their understanding will deepen. They will become active participants in making meaning, discussing ideas, and reflecting on their learning.

It is important to note that the skills that are significant parts of what the arts develop are valued in every field. The arts develop these skills naturally as students explore and translate ideas into artistic form. Researcher Lois Hetland notes, "It is these qualities—intrinsic to the arts—that are valued in every domain but not necessarily taught in those subjects in school. That's what makes the arts such potent resources for teaching valued dispositions—what the arts teach well is not used uniquely in the arts but is valuable across a wide spectrum of contexts" (2009, 37).

Arts and the Standards (*cont.*)

Classroom Environment

A safe classroom environment is needed for social studies ideas and artistic expressions to flourish. Learners must feel comfortable to make mistakes, to critique the work of others, and to celebrate success. Think back to groups to which you have presented new ideas or creative works. How did you feel as you waited for their reactions? What was it about their behavior that made you feel more or less comfortable? What was it about your thinking that made you feel more or less safe? Such reflections will lead you to ways you can talk about these ideas with your students. As teachers, we must be role models for our students as we model our willingness to take risks and engage in new ways of learning. You will find that the arts, by their nature, invite risk taking, experimentation, and self-discipline, as well as encourage the development of a supportive learning community.

Developing a learning community in which learners support and respect one another takes time, but there are things that you can do to help support its development:

- **Establish clear expectations for respect.** Respect is nonnegotiable. As students engage in creative explorations, it is crucial that they honor one another's ideas, invite all voices to the table, and discuss the work in ways that value each contribution. Self-discipline and appreciation for fellow students' creative work is often a beneficial outcome of arts integration (Bellisario and Donovan with Prendergast 2012). Take time for students to brainstorm ways in which they can show one another respect and what they can do when they feel that they have not been respected. Work with students to create guidelines for supporting the creative ideas of others and agree to uphold them as a group.

- **Explore several icebreakers** during the first weeks of school to allow students to get to know one another informally and begin to discover interests they have in common. As students learn more about one another, they develop a sense of themselves as individuals and as a classroom unit and are more apt to want to support one another. Using fun, dynamic warm-ups not only helps students get their brains working but also builds a sense of community and support for risk taking.

- **Tell your students about ways in which you are engaged in learning new ideas.** Talk about your realizations and challenges along the way, and demonstrate your own willingness to take risks and persevere.

- **Find ways to support the idea that we can all act, draw, sing, rhyme, and so forth.** Avoid saying negative things about your own arts or social studies skill levels, and emphasize your continuous growth.

- **Learn to ask questions rather than give answers.** By asking a question like, "What does this symbol represent to you?" students are able to refocus or clarify their own thinking.

Arts and the Standards (*cont.*)

- **Avoid judgments.** Students who are trying to earn your praise for their artistic products will not take the risks necessary for creative work. Encourage students to reflect on their own goals and whether they think they have met them.

- **Emphasize process over product.** Enormous learning and discovery takes place during the creative process. This is as significant as the final product that is produced and in some cases even more so.

How This Book Is Organized

Strategies

The strategies and model lessons in this book are organized within six art modalities:

- creative movement

- drama

- music

- poetry

- storytelling

- visual arts

Within each modality, five strategies are presented that integrate that art form with the teaching of social studies. The strategies are not intended as an exhaustive list but rather as exemplary ways to integrate the arts into social studies.

Though we have provided a model lesson for each strategy, these strategies are flexible and can be used in a variety of ways across a variety of content areas. These models will allow you to try out the ideas with your students and to envision many other ways to adapt these strategies for use in your teaching. For example, we emphasized transportation technology in our creative movement strategy of movement phrases, but you may prefer to integrate it with other areas of social studies, such as demonstrating the perspectives of historical figures. Also, note that many strategies can be implemented across the art forms. For example, the strategy of juxtaposition could be associated with any of the arts as we can juxtapose movements, characters, sounds, words, perspectives, or materials. Furthermore, as you become more familiar and comfortable with the strategies, you may combine a variety of them across the art modalities within one lesson. For example, you might have students begin with creative movement to explore geography, then dramatize landforms and geographic features through tableaux, and finally use those vocabulary words as "found words" to write a poem. The goal is to make the choices that best fit you and your students.

How This Book Is Organized (cont.)

Organization of the Lessons

Each model lesson begins with an **overview**, followed by the list of **standards** addressed. Note that the standards involve equal rigor for both social studies and the arts.

A list of **materials** you will need is provided.

A **preparation** section follows in which ways you can better ensure a successful learning investigation have been identified. Ideas may relate to grouping students, using props to engage learners, or practicing readings with dramatic flair.

The **procedure** section provides step-by-step directions on how to implement the model lesson.

Each model lesson includes **questions** that you can ask as the students work. The questions serve to highlight students' social studies reasoning, stimulate their artistic thinking, or debrief their experience.

How This Book Is Organized *(cont.)*

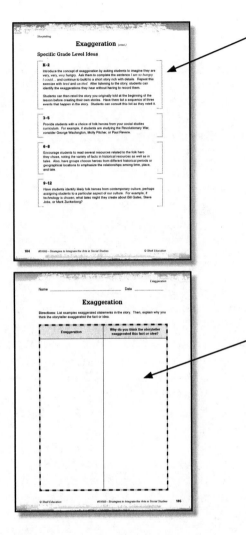

Specific grade level ideas follow with suggestions on how to better meet the needs of students within the K–2, 3–5, 6–8, and 9–12 grade levels. They may also suggest other ways to explore or extend the ideas in the model lesson at these levels. Read all of the sections, as an idea written for a different grade span may suggest something you want to do with your students.

At least one reproducible is provided for each model lesson. Often in the form of graphic organizers, the reproducibles are designed to help students brainstorm ideas, organize and record their thinking, or reflect on their learning. Reproducibles are available on the Digital Resource CD in PDF form and oftentimes as Word documents to allow for customization of content and text for students of diverse abilities and needs.

How This Book Is Organized (cont.)

How to Use the Lessons

These strategies can be used to teach social studies in any K–12 classroom with any social studies curriculum. A model lesson can be implemented as a way to deepen or expand the exploration of a topic, or if you have the flexibility, expanded to several days or a week. You may choose to use the model lesson within your social studies lesson, in combination with time assigned to the arts, or when considering storytelling or poetry, perhaps in conjunction with other content areas.

You may wish to focus on one art form at a time to help yourself become familiar with using that art modality to teach social studies. Or you may want to look through the content index and explore models that relate to what you are teaching now or are about to teach. Over time, you will become familiar with the strategies and find that you choose to integrate them on a regular basis. If integrating the arts and social studies is new to you, consider working with another teacher to explore the ideas together. Collaborate with teachers of art, dance, drama, or music in your school system to draw from their expertise in deepening the artistic work.

You will notice that in many strategies, we encourage you to work with text sets and draw resources from multiple genres and modalities. Mary Ann Cappiello and Erika Thulin Dawes discuss "multimodal, multigenre" text sets (2013, 21), explaining that a text set draws from various modalities, including print, audio, photographs, artifacts, live footage from webcams, and podcasts. By *multigenre*, they suggest diverse forms of writing, such as a blog, in addition to traditional genres, such as books and magazines. Text sets may include nonfiction, fiction, poetry, and more to present a wide view of one topic and the approaches of multiple authors. Primary and secondary sources should be considered with each lesson to provide a wide lens.

In Appendix C: Recommended Resources, you will find multiple suggested text sets based on various historical time periods, such as medieval history, the Civil War, ancient history, and Native American history, to name a few. The text sets, which were developed by Cappiello and Dawes (2013), provide you with a diverse collection of texts from which students can access historical content, providing students with the opportunity to analyze and compare the ways in which social studies content is represented by different points of view.

Assessment

"Data-driven decision making," "documentation of learning," and "meeting benchmarks" are all phrases referring to assessment practices that are embedded in our schools. Assessment has become a time-consuming activity for all involved in education, and yet the time and effort spent does not always yield what is needed to improve learning. As you think about how to assess lessons and activities that integrate social studies and the arts, it is important to stop and consider how to best use assessment to increase learning for your students. It is most likely that in addressing that goal, you will also be documenting learning in ways that can be shared with students, families, administrators, and other interested stakeholders.

How This Book Is Organized (cont.)

We encourage you to focus on formative assessment, that is, assessment that is incorporated throughout the process of learning. This assessment will inform your instructional decisions during the process of teaching. The purpose of this assessment is to provide feedback for learners and teachers along the way in addition to assessment of learning at the end. As such, we are interested in the data collected during the learning process as well as after it is completed. The goals are to make the learning process visible, to determine the depth of understanding, and to note the process students undergo as they translate their social studies knowledge into an art form or explore social studies ideas through artistic explorations.

There are a variety of tools you can use to gather data to support your instructional decision making:

- **Ask questions to draw out, clarify, and probe students' thinking.** The questions in each strategy section will provide you with ideas on which you can elaborate. Use questioning to make on-the-spot adjustments to your plans as well as to identify learning moments as they are unfolding. This can be as simple as posing a new question or as complex as bringing a few students together for a mini-lesson.

- **Walk around with a clipboard or notebook** so that you can easily capture student comments and questions as well as your own observations. Too often, we think we will remember students' words only to find ourselves unable to reproduce them at a later time. These annotations will allow you to note patterns within a student's remarks or among students' comments. They can suggest misconceptions that provide you with an entry to the next day's work through a comment such as, "Yesterday, I noticed that your monologues suggested motivations for your historical figures that were different from what the texts have shared. Let's talk about how this might be possible based on the sources we have and what you have learned about how history is written." A suggested template is provided in Appendix B (page 244) and available on the Digital Resource CD (notetaking.pdf). Make several copies and attach them to a clipboard.

- **Use the graphic organizers in the model lessons** as support for the creative process. Using these forms, have students brainstorm ideas for their artistic process and their social studies connections. These organizers provide a snapshot of students' thinking at a point in the creative process.

- **Use a camera to document student learning.** Each of the strategies leads to a creative product but not necessarily one that provides a tangible artifact or one that fits on a standard-size piece of paper. Use a digital camera to take numerous pictures that can capture, for example, a piece of visual art at various stages of development or the gestures actors and storytellers use in their dramatic presentations. Similarly, use video to capture planning sessions, group discussions, and final presentations. As well as documenting learning, collecting such evidence helps students reflect on their learning. Consider developing a learning portfolio for your students that they can review and add to over time.

How This Book Is Organized (cont.)

- Recognize that although each strategy leads to a final creative product, it, too, can be used to inform future instruction. **Comparisons can be made across products to note student growth.**

- **Make students integral parts of the assessment process.** Provide them with opportunities to reflect on their work. For quick, formative reflections, ask students to respond simply. For example, say, "Move in an unusual way to show a southern direction." Have students reflect in more complex ways as well. For example, have students choose artifacts to include in their portfolio and explain the reasons for their choices. Have students reflect on their work as a class. For example, ask, "How well did we build on one another's ideas today? How well did we support one another's creative thinking?" Encourage discussion of artistic work to not only draw out what students have learned in their own creative process but also how and what they learned from the work of their peers. In this way, students teach and learn from one another.

- **Design rubrics that help you organize your assessment data.** A well-crafted rubric can help you to gather data more quickly as well as increase the likelihood that you are being equitable in your evaluation of assessment data. Select criteria to assess learning in social studies as well as in the art form, because arts integration supports equal rigor in both content and in the arts.

To give you an example of how you might combine these methods, consider the tableaux strategy in the Drama section:

In a third-grade classroom, students were exploring character traits through a lesson about Amelia Earhart. Students read a series of texts based on the life of this groundbreaking female pilot. Next, students were asked to consider text-to-self connections by creating a frozen sculpture with their bodies (the tableaux strategy), showing a character trait that they felt represented some aspect of themselves. This generated a sense of the relevance of character traits and teased out a wide range of personalities and qualities. Students thought hard about what might represent their individual character traits and were thoroughly engrossed in sharing their own traits as well as considering the traits of their peers.

Tableaux
Tableaux Ideas

Name _____ Date _____

Directions: Use the chart to brainstorm ideas in social studies content. Then, list ways you could express your ideas in tableaux.

Character Traits	Ideas for Tableaux (shape, levels, suggested action, relationship between figures)
Caring	Amelia is a nurse's aid helping a wounded pilot in WWI
Independent	Lady Lindy is standing by her plane - shoulders back. Her hand is on the propeller surrounded by a crowd cheering
Fearless	Amelia is in the cockpit of the plane flying through fog. She cannot see but does not panic.

Next, students formed small groups and brainstormed character traits of Amelia Earhart. They analyzed the texts for evidence of a particular character trait, eagerly revisiting the texts as they planned what scene they would create to demonstrate the trait in action. When set to the task, the room was abuzz with conversation about what scene would best bring to life the selected trait. As students made choices about how to bring their ideas to life through tableaux, the conversation moved between ideas about

How This Book Is Organized (*cont.*)

intangible concepts such as bravery and how they ideas could be translated into specific images. Each group created a scene, depicting a moment when the character trait was exemplified. The still images students created included vivid scenes from the texts.

As there are many aspects of this task to capture, a rubric can be quite helpful. A suggested rubric is provided in Appendix B (page 245) and on the Digital Resource CD (assessmentrubric.pdf). Observation protocols help teachers document evidence of student learning, something all teachers must do. A variety of forms can be used and it is not possible to include all areas that you might attend to in an interdisciplinary lesson. Two suggested forms are included in Appendix B, built on the work of Collins (2012a, 2012b) and Dacey (2012a, 2012b, 2012c, 2012d). One form is for use with individual students (page 246, individualform.pdf) and one is for use with groups (page 247, groupform.pdf).

Correlation to the Standards

Correlation to the Standards

Shell Education is committed to producing educational materials that are research and standards based. In this effort, we have correlated all of our products to the academic standards of all 50 United States, the District of Columbia, the Department of Defense Dependent Schools, and all Canadian provinces.

How to Find Standards Correlations

To print a customized correlation report of this product for your state, visit our website at http://www.shelleducation.com and follow the on-screen directions. If you require assistance in printing correlation reports, please contact Customer Service at 1-877-777-3450.

Purpose and Intent of Standards

Legislation mandates that all states adopt academic standards that identify the skills students will learn in kindergarten through grade twelve. Many states also have standards for Pre–K. This same legislation sets requirements to ensure the standards are detailed and comprehensive.

Standards are designed to focus instruction and guide adoption of curricula. Standards are statements that describe the criteria necessary for students to meet specific academic goals. They define the knowledge, skills, and content students should acquire at each level. Standards are also used to develop standardized tests to evaluate students' academic progress. Teachers are required to demonstrate how their lessons meet state standards. State standards are used in the development of all of our products, so educators can be assured they meet the academic requirements of each state.

Common Core State Standards

Many of the lessons in this book are aligned to the Common Core State Standards (CCSS). The standards support the objectives presented throughout the lessons and are provided on the Digital Resource CD (standards.pdf).

McREL Compendium

We use the Mid-continent Research for Education and Learning (McREL) Compendium to create standards correlations. Each year, McREL analyzes state standards and revises the compendium. By following this procedure, McREL is able to produce a general compilation of national standards. Each lesson in this product is based on one or more McREL standards, which are provided on the Digital Resource CD (standards.pdf).

TESOL and WIDA Standards

The lessons in this book promote English language development for English language learners. The standards correlations can be found on the Digital Resource CD (standards.pdf).

Correlation to the Standards *(cont.)*

The main focus of the lessons presented in this book is to promote the integration of the arts in social studies. The standards for both the arts and social studies are provided on the Digital Resource CD (standards.pdf).

Common Core State Standards

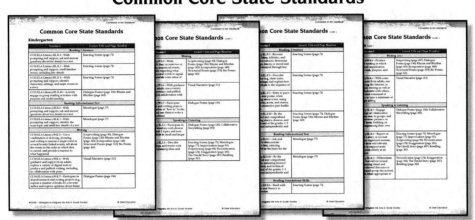

McREL Standards

TESOL and WIDA Standards

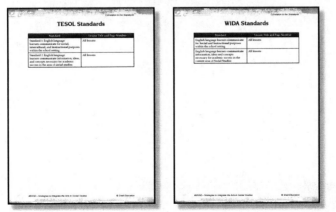

#51092—Strategies to Integrate the Arts in Social Studies

Creative Movement

Creative Movement

Understanding Creative Movement

Integrating creative movement across the curriculum is an engaging approach to teaching that allows students to experience, translate, and communicate social studies concepts kinesthetically. In 1983, Howard Gardner identified bodily-kinesthetic intelligence within his theory of multiple intelligences (2011) as one way that students learn. Neuroscientists are finding that memory and recall are improved when the body is engaged in the learning process (Zull 2002) and that the mind uses the body to make sense of ideas (Carpenter 2010).

While important for all learners, opportunities to express themselves nonverbally can be particularly powerful for some students. Such opportunities can provide students with access to social studies content that would not be possible otherwise. Stacey Skoning states that creative movement, or dance, "is important to incorporate into our inclusive classrooms if we want to meet the needs of more diverse groups of students" (2008, 9).

Creative movement allows students to be physically active, which often increases their attention spans, but it is much more than just the incorporation of movement into classroom activities. When students are involved in creative movement, they become more mindful of their bodies' abilities to communicate, explore what happens when they move with intention, engage in problem solving through movement, and develop awareness of their creative choices. It is important to keep the possibilities for this work in mind as your students explore these model lessons.

As students deconstruct and reconstruct concepts, they take ownership of the ideas through kinesthetic means and creative choices. As choreographer and former elementary school teacher Paula Aarons notes, "figuring out things in your body and through movement weaves ideas together. This builds a sense of intuitive knowledge, of working with an interchange of acting and responding, of physical problem solving" (Aarons, pers. comm. 2012).

Strategies for Creative Movement

✂ Embodiment

In this strategy, students use shapes (body shapes, lines, angles, curves), level (low, middle, high), and movement or gesture to *embody*, or show with their bodies, their understanding of concepts and terms. The strategy can be used to model complex ideas, helping students to grasp, investigate, and internalize concepts. Students can also create spontaneous creative movement to help them summarize or review their learning.

Working with others to embody ideas in movement can prompt students to discuss characteristics of a particular concept, both as they translate ideas into movement and while they view the presentation of other groups' ideas. Dance artist Celeste Miller (Miller, pers. comm. 2012) suggests that the language of movement can provide a "palette for expression of both abstract and tangible ideas." Having groups of students embody the same concept allows students to see how different movement interpretations can convey the same ideas. Coming up with more than one approach for depicting an idea encourages creative and critical thinking. This strategy can help students solidify ideas and help you assess students' depth of understanding.

✂ Moving Statues

This strategy combines held poses with movement as students incorporate the use of shape (body shapes, lines, angles, curves), level (low, medium, high), and quality of movement (characteristics such as sustained, swing, percussive, collapsed), allowing them to make nuanced changes in movements. Students can form moving statues alone, in pairs, or in groups.

A group statue results in a large fluid representation of a concept as students create an evolving model of the idea being explored. Moving statues can also require students to position themselves in relation to others. Through such experiences, creative movement can improve self-esteem and social functioning in addition to deepening understanding of social studies content (Theodorakou and Zervas 2003).

Creative Movement (cont.)

❧ Choreography

Audiences can be mesmerized by dancers moving across the stage alone, in pairs, or in groups. Dancers seem to move seamlessly from individual locations as they join as a group and then part to return to individual spots. Choreographers orchestrate this motion through the planning and notation of movement.

Choreography requires students to decide how to incorporate movements, pathways, tempo, and location into a creative movement piece and then to notate or communicate those decisions. Without such notation, dance instructions could not be transmitted over time (Waters and Gibbons 2004).

❧ Movement Phrases

In this strategy, students create a series of movements to represent the parts of a process or concept. They perform this series of movements, linking each to the next, to illustrate a series of steps or components within a curricular concept. When students link ideas, they can better understand relationships among concepts and form generalizations. As students create and build upon their movement ideas, they also develop the vocabulary of movement such as directional words (pathways) and levels (high, medium, low). According to Stacey Skoning, "having a common movement vocabulary in the classroom benefits everyone because the common vocabulary makes it easier to discuss the movement phrases that are being created" (2008, 6).

❧ Interpretation

In this strategy, students explore and interpret emotion and internal thought processes through abstract movement that symbolizes internal processes. As characters are explored, students embody internal thinking processes, qualities of character traits, and character motivation. Students explore parallels in movement qualities with a variety of emotional states, the qualities of emotion, how things change over time, and how characters' choices can be driven by emotion and character traits.

Embodiment

Model Lesson: Freedom of Expression

Model Lesson Overview

Students use embodiment to explore how sayings and slogans demonstrate freedom of expression and protest and how they communicate values and principles. Students work in groups to physically explore and deepen their understanding of the values and principles communicated through movement, share their ideas with the class, and view the presentations of others.

Standards

K–2

- Knows the state's motto
- Knows the state's slogan
- Moves his or her body in a variety of controlled ways
- Creates shapes at low, middle, and high levels

3–5

- Knows that slogans are a means of expression
- Knows the significance of patriotic sayings that were written long ago
- Creates shapes at low, middle, and high levels
- Uses kinesthetic awareness, concentration, and focus in performing movement skills

6–8

- Knows examples of how an individual's values had an impact on history
- Understands various movements and their underlying principles

9–12

- Analyzes the values held by specific people who influenced history and the role their values played in influencing history
- Understands how movement choices are used to communicate abstract ideas and themes in dance

Materials

- *Embodiment Brainstorming Guide* (page 31, embrainstormingguide.pdf)
- *Observing Others* (page 32, observingothers.pdf)

Embodiment *(cont.)*

Preparation

Prior to this lesson, have students conduct research about patriotic American slogans and sayings, such as "United We Stand," "Home of the Brave," and "Let Freedom Ring." In accordance with the time period you are studying, students can research slogans from the Boston Tea Party, the abolition of slavery, women's suffrage, labor movements, or the civil rights movement. Consider what grouping would be most productive for students to create these embodied representations. Additional ideas are provided in the Specific Grade Level Ideas.

Procedure

1. Model embodiment with the whole class by playing "Answer Me in Movement." Tell students that you are going to say a vocabulary word such as *freedom*, *democracy*, *values*, *principles*, or *protest*. Say, "As I introduce each idea, show me how you understand the concept in movement." You might say, "Freedom," and then say, "Answer me in movement." Students should respond by using their bodies to create shapes or movements that demonstrate their understanding. Students demonstrating their understanding of freedom might move their arms in a sweeping gesture upward and away from their body toward the sky to show joy and the ability to move (speak, act, think) without obstruction. Encourage students to use low, middle, and high levels of space to make their shapes more interesting and to show different directions with the lines their bodies make.

2. Have students compare and contrast the different embodiments. For additional support with more abstract ideas, you can build capacity by giving students more concrete ideas to embody within an idea. For example, open arms could show the democratic principles of including everyone, or arms swinging up to the sky could show the idea of reaching for one's dreams.

3. Discuss with students what a *slogan* is. Ask questions such as, "What is a slogan? What is the purpose of a slogan? What are examples of slogans and sayings from the past? How do slogans and sayings show what people value?"

4. Distribute the *Embodiment Brainstorming Guide* (page 31) activity sheet to students. Have them record slogans or sayings that they discovered in their research, events or ideas that inspired them (including what the people valued), and ways to represent the ideas through creative movement.

Embodiment *(cont.)*

5. Have students break into small groups and choose one of the slogans or sayings from the *Embodiment Brainstorming Guide* to show in movement as a group. Encourage groups to choose a slogan or saying that they would like to understand more fully. Tell groups that they should not share their chosen slogan or saying with other groups so that when they present their movement, classmates can identify the concept being represented. Ask students to distill their ideas into gestural movement in which brief movement choices are used to symbolize big ideas.

6. As students work, check in with each group to provide encouragement, using the Planning Questions to deepen conceptual development. Encourage students to move beyond iconic symbols (e.g., peace symbol shown by holding two fingers up) and explore the meaning of the idea in inventive ways through movement (e.g., *peace* could instead be shown by students moving together with arms linked).

7. Have each group present their embodiment to the rest of the class twice so that the audience has time to take in the details. The viewers can note their observations by using the *Observing Others* (page 32) activity sheet. Ask viewing students to use their observations to help them identify the idea being represented. Use students' observations as a catalyst to spark conversations about the ideas represented.

8. Use the Questions for Discussion to prompt students' reflections on how they translated ideas into movement and what they saw in other groups' embodiments that suggested a particular idea or concept.

Planning Questions

- How might you show the meaning of a slogan or saying with your body?

- What qualities of the slogan or saying are important to share?

- How might you boil down the essence of a slogan or saying into a gesture or embodied movement that represents the qualities of the idea?

Embodiment *(cont.)*

Questions for Discussion

- What ideas did your group identify to translate a slogan or saying into embodied movement?

- How did you translate the ideas into movement?

- What choices did you make in creating movement?

- In what ways did movement help you understand the values and principles of people in the past?

- What struck you about other groups' presentations?

- What ideas do the movements seem to represent?

- What similarities and differences were there in the different movements of the same slogans or sayings?

- Which ideas were challenging to illustrate?

Specific Grade Level Ideas

K–2

To brainstorm a variety of movements, invite students to close their eyes, if they are comfortable, and slowly move their arms any way they wish while staying in the same place. After a minute or so, have students open their eyes and brainstorm and record a list of verbs to describe their movements (e.g., *raise*, *lower*, *bend*, *point*, *circle*, *swing*, and *stretch*). Ask them to demonstrate these movements with different parts of their bodies. Ask them to show you how they would point with their pinkies, legs, or torsos.

Students can use embodiment to understand state mottoes in more depth, such as Texas's motto (Friendship) or Maine's motto (*Dirigo*, meaning "I lead"), or slogans, such as "The Lone Star State" (Texas) and "The Pine Tree State" (Maine). Students can also explore through embodiment the history and significance of American symbols and figures, such as the bald eagle, the Liberty Bell, George Washington as the father of our country, and the national flag. It would also be powerful for students to use embodiment to represent the importance of buildings, statues, and monuments in the state's history and how they memorialize important people and events.

Embodiment *(cont.)*

3–5

In addition to mottoes and slogans, students can also locate songs and poems with similar purposes and messages and distill the essence of these messages through embodiment.

Extend the lesson by exploring the historical significance of the Pledge of Allegiance through embodiment. Students can also research and record famous quotations from important historical figures, such as, "In the truest sense, freedom cannot be bestowed; it must be achieved" (Franklin D. Roosevelt), and express the essence with creative movement.

6–8

Students can research a specific person from history and how the individual's values had an impact on history, showing the values and principles through embodiment. Different groups can choose individuals with opposing views and embody compromises that took place. They can also use embodiment to understand various positions of individuals during religious, philosophical, and social movements of a given time period of study.

9–12

Students can use embodiment to understand various positions of individuals during times of war and oppression. For example, they could demonstrate people's personal reasons for resisting Nazi policies and orders.

Name _____ Date _____

Embodiment Brainstorming Guide

Directions: Brainstorm ideas for using movement to represent the slogan or saying.

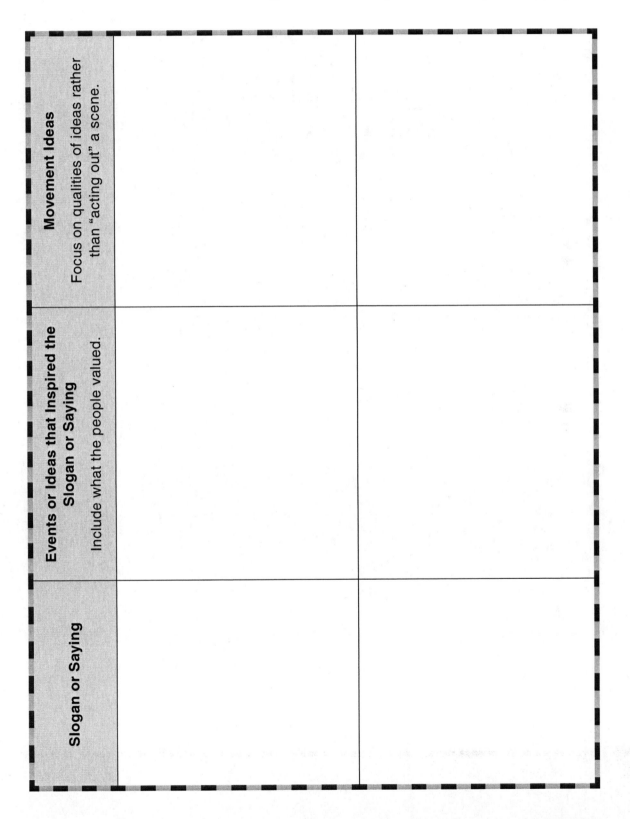

Name _____ Date _____

Observing Others

Directions: As you watch each group perform, record your observations and questions on the chart.

Group Members	What movements did you observe?	What values and principles did the movement suggest? How? Why?	What questions or comments do you have for the artists?

Moving Statues

Model Lesson: Time Lines and Relationships

Model Lesson Overview

In this strategy, students create moving statues to construct and interpret historical data from a time line or to work backward from an issue or event to explain its causes. Half of the class explores the qualities of the events, issues, problems, or causes while the other half observes the movement. Then, the groups switch roles. Finally, students create a group statue that results in a large, fluid representation of a series of historical events or the causes and effects of one event. They position themselves in relation to others to represent ideas and explore the relationships. Students will begin in stillness; bring life to the issue, event, problem, or cause through movement; and then end in stillness.

Standards

K-2

- Distinguishes among broad categories of historical time
- Shows control over body movements
- Creates shapes at low, middle, and high levels

3-5

- Knows how to interpret data presented in time lines
- Identifies and demonstrates movement elements and skills in performing dance
- Creates shapes at low, middle, and high levels

6-8

- Knows how to construct and interpret multiple-tier time lines
- Transfers a spatial pattern from the visual to the kinesthetic
- Reproduces simple movement sequences

Materials

- *Moving through Time* (page 37, throughtime.pdf)

Moving Statues *(cont.)*

Preparation

Determine the time span for your time line and whether students will explore the causes and events leading up to one historical event or many events over time. Think about your students' comfort levels. Should they begin sitting in their chairs, or can they begin standing where they are more visible? Identify how pairs and small groups will be formed: through choice, through a random process such as matching cards, or through your assignment. Also, identify music if you wish to use it. A slow tempo without words is recommended. Additional ideas are provided in the Specific Grade Level Ideas.

Procedure

1. Work with students to create a written time line of events that relates to a period of study you are teaching. Choose an event, issue, problem, or cause to add to the time line. Explain to students that they will enact moving statues as a way to understand the meaning of the events.

2. Have student volunteers model a moving statue by using an event from the time line. Ask students to identify a moment or cause-and-effect relationship to demonstrate through movement. Tell them to begin as frozen statues. Then, have them demonstrate movements that illustrate the event. Encourage students to move beyond a literal acting out of the idea. Rather, they should consider how to represent the ideas in more abstract forms through movement. For example, the beginning of the Civil War might be demonstrated in movement as an elaborate, emotional tug-of-war in slow motion with several movers on both sides, clutching and pulling on an invisible rope. When the movement is done, have students return to frozen statues. Note that beginning and ending with a still image will highlight the qualities of movement.

3. Have the class practice creating moving statues with the events from the class time line. Ask for a volunteer to demonstrate one of the events while the rest of the students are "frozen" as statues. Tell students that when you clap, they will "unfreeze" and activate their statues, demonstrating the events through movement. When you clap twice, they will freeze again. Have a volunteer choose a second event to repeat for practice.

4. Divide the class into several groups. Assign an event on the time line to each group, and have groups create moving statues to show their event. Have groups observe the movements of other groups and record their observations on the *Moving through Time* (page 37) activity sheet. Continue until each student group has interpreted an event.

Moving Statues *(cont.)*

5. Have groups perform their event movements in sequential order to create a group statue that results in a large, fluid representation of a series of historical events or the causes and effects of one event.

6. Debrief with students, using the Questions for Discussion.

Questions for Discussion

- What different movements did you make to represent the event?

- What did you observe about the event as you were watching others share their movement ideas?

- How would you describe the movement used to depict the event? What were the qualities of the movement?

- In what ways did movement help us expand or revise our time line?

Specific Grade Level Ideas

K–2

Select a moment from a time line of events you have identified as a class and ask students to show the emotions and relationships of the individuals through movement. For example, students could show through movement the major events in their local community over time and the emotions associated with them. Have groups of students share moving statues that illustrate different emotions about the same event.

Students can also make a time line of meaningful events and changes in their own lives.

3–5

Create a classroom time line and have students add events to the time line as you read historical fiction or share primary sources, articles, or videos. Share with students the differences between primary and secondary sources. Have students create moving statues to represent different aspects of one event. Students should focus on the multiple perspectives of people involved in the event. For example, students could work with a newspaper article that includes two or more opposing vantage points and create moving statues to illustrate the different perspectives and how they react with each other.

Moving Statues *(cont.)*

6–8

Students can create multiple-tier time lines and view them side-by-side to prompt discussion of multiple facets of a time period or event, including cause-and-effect relationships and other influences. For example, a time line that looks at the settlements in the English, French, and Spanish colonies in North America could be set against a time line of economic developments happening at the same time. Students can focus on turning-point moments when something significant occurred that prompted change and create moving statues to explore these influences.

Name _____ Date _____

Moving through Time

Directions: Observe each group's movement and fill in the chart.

Group Members	Event from the Time Line	Description of Movement Used to Bring it to Life

Choreography

Model Lesson: Maps

Model Lesson Overview

Choreography allows students to explore spatial relationships and directional awareness involved in mapmaking and the natural and human features and places of their community. In small groups, students create a choreography to consider location, distance, and scale in mapmaking. Students focus on the locations and the pathways they follow, and they represent that plan on paper. They can also consider tempo. As students present the choreographed movement, they gain a kinesthetic experience of the mapping process and representations of a map.

Standards

K–2

- Knows the physical and human characteristics of the local community

- Knows the absolute and relative location of a community and places within it

- Moves to the beats, rhythm, and tempo of music

3–5

- Knows major physical and human features of places as they are represented on maps and globes

- Understands the spatial organization of places through such concepts as location, distance, scale, movement, and region

- Uses locomotor movements in different directions

- Uses movements in straight and curved pathways

6–8

- Knows how maps help to find patterns of movement in space and time

- Memorizes and reproduces movement sequences

- Understands various movements and their underlying principles

Materials

- Map of the community

- Musical selections

- Clipboards or drawing paper (*optional*)

- *Movement Pathways* (page 42, pathways.pdf)

- *Choreography Planner* (page 43, choreographyplanner.pdf)

Choreography *(cont.)*

Preparation

It would be ideal to take a walking field trip through the community to experience firsthand the distances between historical sites, shops, rivers, or other important landmarks. You should locate or create a community map that shows the locations of important places in your community. You may also have students draw their own maps to work from. As students plan and perform their movement, use your open meeting area, create open space in the classroom, or plan to use another open space such as the gym or the cafeteria for the creative movement presentations. Provide musical selections for students to choose from, or provide one recording for all students to use during their choreographies. Additional ideas are provided in the Specific Grade Level Ideas.

Procedure

1. Activate students' prior knowledge about the community by asking questions such as, "What are the major physical features in our community? What are the major human features in our community?"

2. If possible, take a walking trip through the community to find important natural and human features. Have students bring a clipboard to sketch a map as they go. If you cannot go on a walking trip, provide students with a simple map of the important locations in your community.

3. Display the term *pathway* and define it as the path a movement or combination of movements can take. Distribute the *Movement Pathways* (page 42) activity sheet to students, which illustrates five possible paths: *straight*, *zigzag*, *curve*, *spiral*, and *circle*. Challenge students to move through open space along these pathways in interesting ways. Ask them to explore all the ways they can move along the path, incorporating such movement choices as levels (high, medium, low), different tempos (fast vs. slow), and using a variety of ways of moving (hopping, twisting, sliding, etc.).

4. Choose two locations in the community for demonstration purposes. Ask students to work in small groups and brainstorm movement ideas to represent traveling from one location to the other. Invite each group to share their favorite movement idea, describe their pathway, and explain their thinking. In addition to physical features and mapping of locations, ask students to consider how they might also capture the character of a place.

5. Explain to students that *choreography* is the combination and planning of movement sequences to make a work that moves together. Note that if a movement phrase is like a sentence, a choreography is like a paragraph. Provide students with the community map to use as they choreograph a dance that shows movement between three locations in their community.

Choreography *(cont.)*

6. Invite students to work in small groups to complete the *Choreography Planner* (page 43) activity sheet. Use the Planning Questions to guide their thinking.

7. If students have drawn their own maps, encourage them to modify their sketches as the process of movement informs their thinking about spatial relationships. For example, they may have discovered during this process that they have drawn locations too close together on their map. Challenge them to consider scale.

8. Invite groups to perform their choreographed work for the class.

9. Debrief using the Questions for Discussion.

Planning Questions

- How might you show the path from one location to the next through movement?

- How can movement help you consider distance and scale?

- How will your movement show the character of a place?

- Where will your movers start?

- What pathways will they follow?

- How will you conclude your choreography?

- How could you add heightened interest to the presentation?

Questions for Discussion

- How did creative movement help you think about the distance and scale of locations on your map?

- Did creative movement help you revise your map? If so, what changes did you make and why?

- What choices did you make in the creation of your choreographed piece?

- What movements suggested a sense of place?

- What did you learn about the physical and human features of your community when watching the choreographies of other groups?

Choreography (cont.)

Specific Grade Level Ideas

K-2

Have students choreograph a dance to explore the spatial elements on a map: locations (points on a map) and transportation and communication routes (lines on a map). They could also create a choreography to represent a map of the playground, a park, or the fire escape routes at or around your school.

3-5

Students can create a choreography to explore the relationships of locations on a historical map from a specific time period. Historical maps can be found on the Library of Congress website. Students can also create choreographies to represent a map located inside a historical fiction text.

6-8

Students can create a choreography to represent the mapping of hurricane tracks over several seasons, the spread of influenza throughout the world, or other patterns of movement in space and time. Choreography can help students explore data on population distribution, language-use patterns, or energy consumption at different times of the year. They could also create a choreography to show the location of physical and human features on maps and globes—cultural hearths such as Mesopotamia, Huang Ho, the Yucatan Peninsula, the Nile Valley, or major ocean currents, wind patterns, landforms, and climate regions.

Name _____ Date _____

Movement Pathways

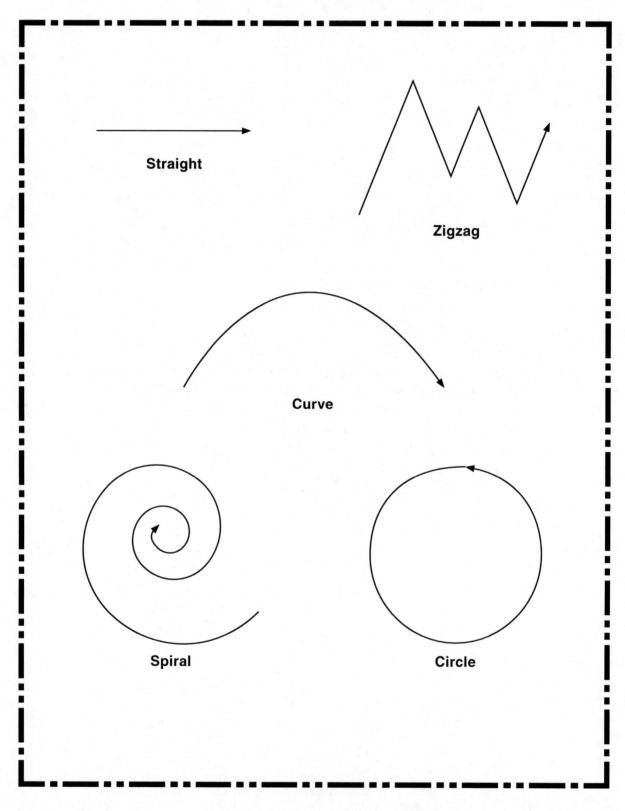

Name _____ Date _____

Choreography Planner

Directions: Use this sheet to plan movements between features in your community for your choreography.

> **Physical or human feature in our community #1**
>
> _____

> **Movement to show the distance and direction to the next location**
>
> _____
>
> _____
>
> _____

> **Physical or human feature in our community #2**
>
> _____

> **Movement to show the distance and direction to the next location**
>
> _____
>
> _____
>
> _____

> **Physical or human feature in our community #3**
>
> _____

Movement Phrases

Model Lesson: Transportation Technology

Model Lesson Overview

In this strategy, students use movement phrases to explore how transportation technology has connected places and affected relationships over time. Groups focus on the qualities of movement and movement transitions between ideas, working together to perform their movement phrases in sequential order to show progression over time. Note that students are exploring the characteristics of these ideas and relationships through movement rather than "acting out" the history of advancements.

Standards

K–2

- Knows the modes of transportation used to move people, products, and ideas from place to place
- Uses kinesthetic awareness, concentration, and focus in performing movement skills
- Knows basic actions and movement elements, and how they communicate ideas

3–5

- Understands how changing transportation technology has affected relationships between locations
- Uses locomotor movements in different directions
- Uses movements in straight and curved pathways

6–8

- Understands how the connections between places demonstrates interdependence
- Understands how the connections between places demonstrates accessibility
- Knows a range of dynamics/ movement qualities
- Understands the action and movement elements observed in dance, and knows appropriate movement/dance vocabulary

9–12

- Understands how communication and transportation technologies contribute to cultural convergence or divergence (e.g., convergence created by electronic media, computers, and jet aircraft; divergence created by technologies used to reinforce nationalistic or ethnic elitism or cultural separateness and independence)
- Understands how movement choices are used to communicate abstract ideas and themes in dance

Movement Phrases *(cont.)*

Materials

- *Six Qualities of Movement Reference Sheet* (pages 49–50, qualitiessheet.pdf)

- *Transportation Technology Effects* (page 51, transporteffects.pdf)

Preparation

Prior to this lesson, students should become familiar with the time line of events in transportation technology according to your curriculum's local, regional, or world studies. Determine the time period and mode of transportation that you would like each group to study. You may have groups show the same technologies or different technologies. Locate and bookmark primary sources, such as photographs on the Library of Congress website, to share with students. Contact your local historical society for information about transportation technology in your community over time and how and why the community was accessible to people from prehistory through today. Additional ideas are provided in the Specific Grade Level Ideas.

Procedure

1. Share with students primary sources related to transportation technology (as appropriate for the grade level and curriculum). Tell students that they will explore the impact of transportation technology through movement phrases.

2. Explain to students that they will create a series of connected movements called *movement phrases* and that these sequences should represent the impact of transportation technology. Explain that a movement phrase is a series of connected movements that conveys an idea, much like a sentence is a series of connected words that conveys an idea. Students' movement phrases can show ideas related to changes in trade, where people lived, the work they did, and the inventions that resulted. Have students brainstorm ideas about how they can use movement to represent the cause-and-effect relationships of transportation technology on society. Work from a specific example that students have been studying, such as the Erie Canal, and encourage students to try out movement ideas after discussing them.

3. Distribute the *Six Qualities of Movement Reference Sheet* (pages 49–50) to students and discuss the qualities with students. Note that the goal is not to have students memorize this list but to offer them new ways of thinking about how a movement can be executed and communicated in nuanced ways. Allow time for students to make various movements, applying different movement qualities to them. Have students explore different combinations of movements and qualities and take notes about what they found worked well together.

Movement Phrases *(cont.)*

4. Divide students into groups. Have each group complete the *Transportation Technology Effects* (page 51) activity sheet as they plan their movement phrases, using their notes as a starting point for selecting movements.

5. Encourage students to explore different combinations of movements before they make final choices. Use the Planning Questions to guide their thinking. Ask students to be aware of the conversations they have during this process as they translate ideas into movement. Have students identify how they will use creative movement to transition from one component to the next.

6. Allow students time to explore their choices physically and to rehearse their movement phrases until they are ready to present to the class.

7. Have groups present their movement phrases to the class. Ask students to begin and end in stillness in order to heighten the experience for viewers.

8. Ask the viewers to observe the movement presentations closely and identify the ideas being portrayed, noting the movement choices made. Use the Questions for Discussion to prompt students' reflections on the process of translating ideas into movement and on what viewers saw in the movement phrases that suggested the characteristics of ideas.

Planning Questions

- How might you use movement to show how transportation connects locations?

- How will you show the following changes: what people traded, where people lived, what they did for work, and what they invented?

- What might this look like as ideas are linked together in a sequence?

- How might you connect these ideas in smooth transitions so that one movement idea flows into the next?

- How does your movement sequence communicate like a sentence?

Movement Phrases *(cont.)*

Questions for Discussion

- What did you learn about the impact of transportation technology during the process of translating ideas into movement?

- What choices did your group make in the creation of the movement phrase?

- How did the group presentation allow you to understand how transportation technology has connected locations over time?

- In what ways did movement phrases help you understand cause-and-effect relationships?

- How might the experience of movement phrases help you consider future relationships with new innovations?

Specific Grade Level Ideas

K–2

Students can use movement phrases to explore one concept as a class, such as the impact of the Erie Canal. Have students view primary sources, such as photographs from the Library of Congress website, to explore how the transportation technology of the Erie Canal changed trade in the interior of the country, allowed access to The Finger Lakes, shifted where people lived, changed what they did for work, shifted how agrarian communities and factories were linked, and allowed for inventions such as McCormick's Reaper because of expanded trade routes in addition to the steamboat and the sewing machine.

Students can use movement phrases to explore the modes of transportation used to move people, products, and ideas from place to place, such as barges, airplanes, automobiles, pipelines, ships, and railroads, focusing on the advantages and disadvantages of each.

Students can also explore the cause-and-effect relationships involved with the decisions made by significant historical figures of the community or the reasons why different groups immigrated to a state or region.

Movement Phrases *(cont.)*

3–5

Have students use what they learned from movement phrases to explore how present day transportation technology such as airplanes and trains affect relationships. Students could use movement phrases to represent how transportation and communication technologies have evolved. For example, they can explore how transportation and communication have changed and affected trade and economic activities such as improved roads and refrigerated trucking, more fresh fruits and vegetables available out of season, and the expansion of regional, national, and global markets as transportation and communication systems improve.

6–8

Have students use movement phrases to represent the dependence over time of Americans on other regions and countries for imported resources and manufactured goods and issues of interdependence and accessibility. Also, have students explore the relationship between transportation technology and communication technology. As transportation technologies have developed over time, how have communication technologies become important? Have students debate through movement phrases: In what ways have technological and communication advances brought people closer together or farther apart?

9–12

Students can analyze how advancements in transportation technologies can reinforce and contribute to feelings of nationalism or cultural divergence when exploring the impact of German U-boats first used during World War I. Have students use movement to explore President Woodrow Wilson's decision to enter into the war after the sinking of the *Lusitania* and how unprecedented submarine warfare further contributed to the United States' decision to oppose the Central Powers alliance of Austria-Hungary and Germany. Students should use movement to express the sentiments felt by supporters and opponents of the war (e.g., the sentiments of soldiers, women, children, politicians, organizations, or activists). Students can also explore how improved means of communication also contributed to the war effort (e.g., how the Zimmerman Telegram also prompted the United States to declare war on Germany). Students can use their bodies to create movement phrases that communicate the United States' reaction to the Zimmerman Telegram and how news of Germany's plans to create an alliance with Mexico served as a catalyst for U.S. entry into World War I.

Six Qualities of Movement
Reference Sheet

Percussive:

Percussive movements are quick, forceful, and sudden. They are broken up by quick pauses. Think of someone suddenly stomping his or her feet and pausing briefly afterward to increase the impact of the movement.

Sustained:

Sustained movements are flowing, ongoing, and smooth. Think of sliding your foot out away from your body in a long, fluid push.

Vibratory:

Vibratory movements are similar to percussive ones, but they are quicker and less forceful. The movements could involve tapping or shaking.

Six Qualities of Movement
Reference Sheet *(cont.)*

Suspension:

A suspension movement is the slight pause that occurs between motions. The pause can draw attention to the movement just before or after.

Collapse:

Collapse movements give in to the pull of gravity. They can be sudden movements, such as a quick fall to the floor, or they can be gradual motions, such as the controlled lowering of your leg.

Swing/Pendular:

A swing or pendular movement goes back and forth. An example would be an arm that swings up high, pauses briefly, and then returns back down.

Name _____ Date _____

Transportation Technology Effects

Directions: Work with your group to complete the chart and explore transportation technology and how it has connected locations and affected relationships.

Transportation Ideas and Relationships	Movement Ideas and Qualities	What transitions will you create to link these movements?
Transportation Technology: Describe the advancement.		
Locations Connected by the Technology: Name the cities, regions, and/or countries connected.		
Impacts on the People: Describe how this technology changed the lives of people (e.g., trade, settlements, work, inventions).		

Interpretation

Model Lesson: Community Problems and Perspectives

Model Lesson Overview

In this lesson, students explore the problems of their community's past and use interpretive movement to understand the differing perspectives involved in solving them. These movements may include wide arm swings or other movement that occurs from a stationary position (axial movement), movement from one place to another (locomotor movement), moving through space in a variety of directions (pathways), and interesting placement of shapes in space (low, medium, or high levels). Students also use movement to choose different courses of action and infer how events might have turned out differently in their community.

Standards

K–2

- Understands changes in community life over time

- Creates shapes at low, middle, and high levels

- Improvises, creates, and performs dances based on personal ideas and concepts from other sources

3–5

- Knows that community members offered different perspectives on problems the community encountered

- Knows the choices community members had when the community encountered problems

- Knows how ideas are communicated through movement elements

- Knows basic actions and movement elements and how they communicate ideas

6–8

- Predicts how events might have turned out differently in one's local community if specific individuals or groups had chosen different courses of action

- Understands various movements and their underlying principles

- Understands the action and movement elements observed in dance, and knows appropriate movement/dance vocabulary

Interpretation *(cont.)*

Materials

- *Movement Suggestions* (page 56, movesuggestions.pdf)
- *Differing Perspectives* (page 57, differing.pdf)

Preparation

Contact your local historical society and find out about what problems and possible solutions have occurred in the history of your local community. Have students research individuals and groups who offered different perspectives. Gather primary sources such as letters, photographs, and sketches to share with students. Additional ideas are provided in the Specific Grade Level Ideas.

Procedure

1. Ask students how they might show a particular trait or emotion through movement. Work through an example such as, "How might you show anger through movement? How would you describe the quality of the movement that depicts this emotion?"

2. Discuss with students different qualities of movement. For example, students can stay in one place and swing their arms (axial movement) or move through space (pathways). They can vary the speed and timing of their movements as well as the sharpness or fluidity. They can also use their bodies to make shapes at different levels (low, medium, or high).

3. Talk with students about how emotions can inform the way we interpret perspectives that are different from our own. Work through a series of emotions and have students experiment with movement ideas, describing the kinds of movement that best capture the essence of the emotion. As a class, use the *Movement Suggestions* (page 56) activity sheet to develop a list of movement ideas that students can work from as they move forward.

4. Ask students, "Can you think of a time in your life when you had to compromise your opinion or perspective? How did you feel while expressing your opinion? How did you feel when compromising? How can you show that change in emotion through movement?" Discuss examples of when students may experience this kind of change in emotion. Ask students to pick two emotions and demonstrate how they move from one emotion to another, illustrating the transition through movement.

Interpretation *(cont.)*

5. Explain to students that they will work in small groups to explore the different perspectives of community members of the past and their views on solving problems by using interpretive movement. Use the Planning Questions to prompt students to consider emotional shifts in your community. Make a list of motivations and emotions that are suggested by the problem(s) of the past for students to reference throughout the lesson.

6. Divide students into groups according to different community perspectives. Have groups complete the *Differing Perspectives* (page 57) activity sheet and create interpretive movements. If desired, groups may refer to the completed *Movement Suggestions* activity sheet for ideas.

7. Allow time for students to practice their movements.

8. Invite groups to perform their interpretations one after another to portray through movement the different perspectives of the community members or groups.

9. Gather the class and reflect on the process using the Questions for Discussion.

Planning Questions

- What problems has our community encountered in the past?

- What choices did community members have to make to solve the problems?

- What solutions did community members choose and why?

- What movements might express differing perspectives? What movements might express compromise?

- What emotions may have emerged in the solving of the dilemma? Why?

- How may emotion have influenced outcomes?

Questions for Discussion

- How did movement help you explore differing perspectives?

- How did interpretation help you understand a compromise?

- What did you notice about the shifts in emotion portrayed as the groups performed their work?

- Describe the movement qualities you observed that showed particular perspectives.

- How did you recognize a particular perspective?

Interpretation (cont.)

Specific Grade Level Ideas

K–2

Students can use interpretive movement to understand changes in the local community over time. For example, they can explore changes in goods and services, changes in architecture and landscape, or even changes in jobs, schooling, transportation, communication, religion, or recreation. Students can also focus on one or more historical figures in the community and their perspectives on solving problems.

3–5

Extend the lesson by having students compare and contrast the problems and solutions of the past with today's problems and solutions. How are today's issues similar to and different from problems of the past? Have students explore the comparisons through movement. Encourage students to find and represent compromises.

6–8

Have students use interpretive movement to imagine how events might have turned out differently if individuals or groups had chosen different courses of action. Students should also expand the realm of study from community problems to world history, using interpretation to explore the thinking and differing perspectives of social movements and political parties. Students can also represent the different perspectives of characters in a historical fiction text, such as Thomas Jefferson, Sally Hemings, Jefferson's enslaved children, his white children, and the enslaved individuals on his plantation.

Name _____ Date _____

Movement Suggestions

Directions: Describe possible movements that embody each emotion.

Emotion	Movement Descriptions
Anger	
Fear	
Jealousy	
Love	
Worry	
Disgust	
Hope	
Caring	

Name _____ Date _____

Differing Perspectives

Directions: Answer the following questions with your group.

1. What was the problem in the community?

   _____

   _____

   _____

   _____

2. What were the different perspectives on solving the problem?

   _____

   _____

   _____

   _____

   _____

3. How might you express each perspective through movement?   How would you express a compromise through movement?

   _____

   _____

   _____

   _____

   _____

Drama

Drama

Understanding Drama

Integrating drama into the social studies classroom can deepen students' connections with social studies and foster students' ability to find relevance in their own lives and interests. Drama can provide engaging contexts for bringing stories to life. As students embody characters, they imagine themselves in the context of a story. They inhabit perspectives other than their own and experience a character or story from inside the story world. Students examine why characters make particular choices and how stories unfold in specific ways. Through this process, students experience story elements emotionally and physically.

As students explore the dramatization of scenarios, they uncover and deepen their comprehension skills. They make personal connections to fiction and nonfiction texts, investigate characterization, and identify real-world connections. Christopher Andersen (2004) notes that drama has the ability to re-create the essential elements in the world. In roles, students must make choices, solve problems, translate concepts, and articulate ideas. This process requires students to explain, persuade, clarify, and negotiate their thinking (Elliott-Johns et al. 2012). As students investigate perspectives that are different from their own, they expand their worldviews and develop an awareness of their own. Such experiences help students clarify their thinking, understand different perspectives, and consider new strategies for solving problems.

The use of drama in social studies can bring forward multiple perspectives on events, choices, and dilemmas across the globe. Through scenes and character development, students can examine voices that have been marginalized or that are missing, moving beyond acceptance of dominant perspectives that have been typically taught over time. This can anchor work in primary and secondary sources, including oral histories and primary source photographs. Consider the complexities and the sensitivities involved in enacting issues of the past and questioning the perspectives that have framed history in more dominant views. Students will need to be able to engage in critiquing and questioning who is telling the story and what voices are missing. Teachers and students will need to be aware of their own frames of reference and the likelihood that they will encounter stereotypical representations that need to be challenged and confronted as they investigate the unheard voices and marginalized groups throughout history.

Drama (cont.)

Strategies for Drama

✒ Tableaux

Sometimes called image theater or human sculpture, *tableau* is a French word meaning "frozen picture." It is a drama technique that allows for the exploration of an idea without movement or speaking. In this strategy, students use their bodies to create a shape or a full picture to tell a story, represent a concept literally, or create a tangible representation of an abstract concept. Working with physical stance (low, medium, high), suggested relationships (body placement and eye contact), and a sense of action frozen in time allows students to explore ideas and provides a range of ways for students to share what they know about a concept. One person can create a frozen image, or a group can work together to create an image. The process of creating group tableaux prompts discussion of the characteristics of what is being portrayed. The learning occurs in the process of translating ideas to physical representation. Tableaux can also be used as a way to gain entry into a complex idea or bigger project (Walker, Tabone, and Weltsek 2011).

✒ Enacting Scenes

The bread-and-butter of drama is the development and enactment of scenes. Students portray characters who find themselves in particular settings and who are influenced by specific circumstances. They make choices, solve problems, and react to relationships with other characters. We watch (or participate) as characters make choices and deal with implications. Scenes are valuable thinking frames and can be used flexibly across content and contexts. Studies suggest that learning through drama benefits comprehension, including increased confidence with speaking, listening, fluency, and working with complex language (Brouillette and Jennings 2010). Drama integration supports writing skills in terms of focus, use of details, and the navigation of meaning through the consideration of multiple perspectives (Cremin et al. 2006). Students can enter a suggested scene or create their own in response to a particular historical event or issue within social studies themes.

This process of acting out a text provides a meaningful opportunity for students to go back through the text and reread parts that were not clear, visualize elements in the story, and consider the choices made, the role of context, circumstance, and character motivation. Students imagine a character coming to life, question what they are reading, and check for story elements in a natural, purposeful manner. This metacognition, or being aware of the reading strategies as they are used, leads students to a deeper understanding of the text.

Drama (cont.)

❧ Monologue

A *monologue* is a dramatic scene performed by one person. In creating a monologue, students take the perspective of a character in a story, real or imagined, and speak directly to the audience for one to three minutes. The character must be established without interactions with others (that would be a dialogue) and must speak in a way that engages the audience with this singular focus.

There are often monologues in stories and plays that illuminate what a character is thinking. Most often, a monologue reveals a conflict of some kind that the character is wrestling with, a choice to be made, or a problem to be solved. Note that variations include *soliloquy* in which a character is speaking to him or herself. The creation of a monologue provides the opportunity to investigate what Barry Lane calls a "thoughtshot" of a character's inner thinking (1992).

This strategy allows students to "get into the head" of a particular character. Eventually, the goal is for students to create their own monologues, but you may want to introduce the strategy by having students explore prepared ones in resources such as *Magnificent Monologues for Kids 2: More Kids' Monologues for Every Occasion!* by Chambers Stevens and *Minute Monologues for Kids* by Ruth Mae Roddy. Then, students can develop characters and create and perform monologues for inanimate objects or forces, or they can portray specific characters (a historical figure, a character from a book, a newspaper article, or a painting, or they can create an imagined character). In order for a monologue to be dramatic, the character must have some tension or conflict that he or she is wrestling with. This conflict can be an internal or external dilemma. Its resolution or the naming of it will create dramatic interest.

❧ Improvisation

A foundation of drama, improvisation is when individuals create a scene or dramatization "in the moment," making it up as they go. This kind of drama unfolds in exciting and often unpredictable ways as circumstances and character motivation come together to influence how a scene progresses. Improvisation can develop divergent thinking, language use, and social skills, while allowing students to test ideas in a situation that is safe but feels real.

❧ Scriptwriting

In scriptwriting, students write a scene or a set of scenes to create a short theatrical piece with a clear beginning, middle, and end. The focus is on dialogue and the interaction between characters within a clear arc of a story. The drama is driven by dramatic tension and characters who have specific motivations. These motivations drive characters' choices as they move toward what they want or need and create interesting interactions between characters through dialogue and action. Scripts can be collaboratively developed. Having students improvise first and write later encourages free-form dialogue that can then be edited and shaped into a coherent story.

Tableaux

Model Lesson: Voluntarism

Model Lesson Overview

In this lesson, students create *tableaux*, or statues, to explore the roles of voluntarism in society and the charitable, religious, and civic services in their own communities, state, nation, and the world, without moving or speaking. Students choose a cause or explore the visions of an organized group and represent ideas through tableaux.

Standards

K-2

- Knows that responsibility can be a duty to do something
- Knows some of the benefits of fulfilling responsibilities
- Engages in fantasy dramatic play
- Selects interrelated characters, environments, and situations for simple dramatizations

3-5

- Understands that people should volunteer to help others in their family, schools, communities, state, nation, and the world
- Understands that volunteering is a source of individual satisfaction and fulfillment
- Knows characters in dramatizations, their relationships, and their environments
- Knows how visual elements (e.g., space, color, line, shape, texture) and aural aspects are used to communicate locale and mood

6-8

- Knows factors that have influenced American voluntarism
- Knows services that are provided by charitable, religious, and civic groups in the community
- Knows volunteer opportunities that exist in one's own school and community
- Creates characters, environments (e.g., place, time, atmosphere/ mood), and actions that create tension and suspense

9-12

- Understands the roles of voluntarism and organized groups in American social and political life
- Understands the validity and practicality of cultural, historical, and symbolic information used in making artistic choices for informal and formal productions

Tableaux *(cont.)*

Materials

- Primary and secondary sources to show the history of voluntarism
- *Tableaux Ideas* (page 69, tableauxideas.pdf)
- *Gallery Walk Observation Sheet* (page 70, gallerywalk.pdf)

Preparation

As you prepare to use this strategy to explore voluntarism, think about how to group students so that more complex ideas can be represented fully (see step 5 of the Procedure for suggested grouping). Select concepts and identify group size before beginning. As this strategy involves physical interaction, review respectful ways to work together and respect space. Use primary sources, such as photographs and letters, and secondary sources to show historical moments in voluntarism. Additional ideas are provided in the Specific Grade Level Ideas.

Procedure

1. Tell students that *tableaux* means "frozen pictures." Introduce what a tableau is by inviting two students to join you in creating a tableau for the word *bridge*. Dramatize being a sculptor as you "mold" the students into a bridge. Do this by describing how you want them to position their bodies or by modeling for them so that they can mirror what you do. For example, to make the bridge, you could ask students to face each other, bend forward, extend arms, and then hold hands. Have students make a bridge in several different ways.

2. As students create bridges, ask the viewers to describe what they see. Note the words that students suggest (e.g., students may suggest *connect*, *span*, and *arch*). Discuss the idea that each word has a literal meaning but also works figuratively.

3. Ask students to work in groups of three or four to create a tableau that expresses a figurative meaning of the word *bridge*. They can create a caption (written or spoken) that demonstrates the idea they have created (e.g., "The support of my friend created a bridge to a new life."). They can share this caption verbally during their presentation or write the caption on paper and display it.

4. Have students share their tableaux and discuss the experience as a class.

Tableaux *(cont.)*

5. Tell students that they will use tableaux to understand concepts about voluntarism, such as the mission of the American Red Cross. Choose from among the following grouping options:

- Have students work in pairs. One student is the "sculptor" and the other is "clay." The sculptor molds the clay into a human sculpture representing the idea.

- Have students work in small groups. One or two group members go to the center of the room and begin the sculpture with a physical pose. The rest of the participants "add on" one by one to create a group sculpture until all group members are involved.

- For more complex ideas, students can create a "slide show" in which they create multiple tableaux that show a progression. Images are presented one right after the other. Viewers can share their thinking about what they have seen following each slide show.

6. Distribute the *Tableaux Ideas* (page 69) activity sheet to groups. Provide time for groups to develop their ideas and rehearse their tableaux. Have students mine primary and secondary sources for evidence of voluntarism to include in their tableaux.

7. Have groups present their tableaux during a "gallery walk" in which the class views each group's work. You might introduce this by saying, "Imagine we are in an art gallery. We will walk around and look at the sculptures. At each stop on our gallery walk, we will talk about what we see and brainstorm words we think of and how what we see in the tableau suggests voluntarism." Depending on the way the tableaux have developed, sculptors could demonstrate the way they molded the clay, or students could just get into formation. Distribute the *Gallery Walk Observation Sheet* (page 70) activity sheet to students and have them record their observations. Use the Questions for Discussion to guide students' thinking.

8. As a class, review the words and phrases they wrote to describe each tableau, and record them for the class to see. This list of adjectives, synonyms, and metaphors will allow students to understand the concept in new ways. Next, challenge students to list antonyms to the words they have brainstormed. Add to the list as each group describes their process of creating tableaux. This is often where ideas are translated and realizations occur. Capturing students' language will reveal the connections they have made and will draw out questions for further exploration.

Tableaux (cont.)

Questions for Discussion

For the viewers:

- What concept do you think is being represented?

- What words or phrases come to mind as you view the tableaux?

- What do you see in the sculptures that suggested the idea of voluntarism?

- What actions are suggested?

- How does all this information influence your interpretation of the tableaux?

- What similarities and differences were there in the tableaux?

For the participants:

- Describe your process for creating an image that captured the essence of the concept.

- What was the sculpting experience like?

- How did the process help you to more deeply understand the idea of voluntarism?

- What was it like to join the tableau?

Specific Grade Level Ideas

K–2

Invite students to explore more concrete terms that can be clearly demonstrated through tableaux, such as emotions, actions, or structures. For example, students can explore the term *satisfaction* or how they feel when they volunteer. Students can also use tableaux to understand how certain character traits enhance a citizen's ability to fulfill personal and civic responsibilities such as *trustworthy*, *caring*, or *helpful*.

3–5

In addition to ideas about voluntarism, students can also use tableaux to explore issues about personal, political, and economic rights. For example, students can create a tableau to represent the economic right to choose one's work. Students can also use tableaux to understand contemporary issues about rights, such as equal pay for equal work or reciting prayer in schools.

Tableaux *(cont.)*

6–8

Students can debate the importance of service and represent their key points through tableaux. They can also use tableaux to explore issues about personal, political, and economic rights. For example, they can show qualities and ideas about the right to vote, the right to run for public office, freedom of speech, press, assembly, petition, etc. Group tableaux can show ideas about economic rights such as the right to join a labor union or a professional association.

9–12

Students can create a group tableau that expresses the voluntarism behind the creation of the Underground Railroad. Have one student serve as the sculptor, working with students to create formations that capture the reasons and motivations behind the creation of the Underground Railroad. The tableau should express how the Underground Railroad was organized in response to a social need for abolition and emancipation in America. Students can explore how Harriet Tubman and other individuals sympathetic to the abolitionist cause may have felt as they helped free fugitive slaves through an organized network of safe houses and escape routes that led to free states and Canada. As students create a group tableau, they should consider the relationships among fugitive slaves, abolitionists, supporters of slavery, government, religious groups, and the policies of other countries.

Name _____ Date _____

Tableaux Ideas

Directions: Use the chart to brainstorm ideas about voluntarism. Then, list ways you could express your ideas in tableaux.

Ideas about Voluntarism	Ideas for Tableaux (shape, levels, suggested action, relationship between figures)
A cause or need in the community, state, nation, or world:	
An organized volunteer group and its mission:	
A charitable, religious, or civic service and the people who are helped:	

Name _____   Date _____

Gallery Walk Observation Sheet

Directions: Use the chart to record notes as you observe the tableaux.

Observation Notes	Tableau 1	Tableau 2	Tableau 3
What do you notice? (words to describe the tableaux)			
What artistic choices did the participants make? (choices of the "sculptor" and "clay" during the process)			
How did they represent key ideas?			
What have you learned about the concept through tableaux? How does it apply to your everyday life?			

Enacting Scenes

Model Lesson: Historical Fiction

Model Lesson Overview

In this lesson, students act out scenes from historical fiction, taking on the roles of specific characters or ideas. As they plan for their enactment, students use reading strategies such as rereading and scanning for clarification. Finally, students view the scenes of their peers and consider how the stories compare and contrast with information from nonfiction sources.

Standards

K–2

- Understands the contributions and significance of historical figures in the community
- Knows various ways of staging classroom dramatizations
- Plans and prepares improvisations

3–5

- Knows of problems in the community's past, the different perspectives of those involved, the choices people had, and the solutions they chose
- Understands changes in land use and economic activities in the local community since its founding
- Plans visual and aural elements for improvised and scripted scenes
- Understands the visual, aural, oral, and kinetic elements of dramatic performances

6–8

- Understands that specific individuals and the values those individuals held had an impact on history
- Organizes rehearsals for improvised and scripted scenes

Materials

- Historical fiction text of choice
- Props or supplies for students to make props (*optional*)
- *Drama Planner* (page 75, dramaplanner.pdf)
- *Reading Reflection* (page 76, readingreflection.pdf)

Enacting Scenes *(cont.)*

Preparation

Decide if you would like student groups to write original historical scenes to enact or use improvisation in which they re-create the scene on the spot. Also, decide if you would like each group to choose a historical fiction text or if you would like groups to enact different scenes from the same text. If desired, gather props or supplies for students to make props to allow for rich characters.

In the days and weeks prior to the lesson, have students view and read nonfiction literature and other sources that provide historically accurate accounts, as they will be comparing and contrasting information presented in historical fiction and nonfiction. Additional ideas are provided in the Specific Grade Level Ideas.

Procedure

1. Tell students that they will be enacting scenes from a historical fiction story. Read aloud or review your chosen historical fiction text.

2. Divide students into small groups and have each group choose a scene to enact. Distribute the *Drama Planner* (page 75) activity sheet to students in each group.

3. Discuss the reading strategies that students may find themselves using as they prepare to enact their scene: rereading, scanning for important information, visualizing the characters, considering story elements, visualizing scenes as they create a beginning, middle, and end, and using prior knowledge. Distribute the *Reading Reflection* (page 76) activity sheet to students and direct them to check off the strategies as they use them.

4. Provide time for students to work in small groups to complete the *Drama Planner* activity sheet and rehearse their scenes, improvising action and dialogue from what they remember about the story. Monitor groups and use the Planning Questions to help students prepare for the dramatizations. Point out reading strategies as you observe them being used or hear them being discussed, reminding students to check them off on the *Reading Reflection* activity sheet.

5. If desired, provide students with props or supplies to make props for use in their scenes.

6. Have each group enact their scene for the class. Debrief with students about the process, using the Questions for Discussion. Ask students to compare the historical fiction scenes with what they know about the actual historical events. Encourage students to reference factual information presented in various nonfiction texts.

Enacting Scenes *(cont.)*

Planning Questions

- How will you begin and end your scene?

- What interesting action might take place as the plot unfolds?

- Besides the identified characters in the story, are there other historical objects/forces in the story that can be created as characters?

- How will you show what your character wants in the scene?

- What choices will you use in depicting your character (voice, movement, props)?

- How will you show the significance of the historical moment?

Questions for Discussion

- What did you notice in the scenes that made you think differently about what you had read?

- What influenced the decision or action that unfolded in the scene?

- What other endings to your scene can you imagine? How might you change outcomes of the historical event?

- What reading strategies did you use to draw upon information from the text in planning for your scenes?

- What advice would you give a classmate for creating new scenes in the future?

- In what ways did enacting scenes affect your understanding of the time period?

- In what ways did enacting scenes help you compare a fictional story to a nonfiction account?

Enacting Scenes (cont.)

Specific Grade Level Ideas

K–2

Students can work from stories about life in a pioneer farming community, such as *My Community Long Ago* by Bobbie Kalman. Have them enact a scene as you read it aloud. Provide students with time to create props to help the meaning come alive. If desired, work through the beginning, middle, and end of the scene as a class.

3–5

Students can read a picture book such as *Those Rebels, John and Tom* by Beverly Kerley to learn about the personalities, character traits, and compromises of the founding fathers. Have students use improvisation in enacting a scene to explore the significance of compromise. Students can add additional scenes that are not in the book but could have happened. Once complete, they can document their enactments in writing, noting the back-and-forth dialogue and description of action.

Students can read historical fiction texts about the challenges and difficulties encountered by people in pioneer farming communities or the changes in land use and economic activities in the local community since its founding.

Consider having students enact a scene from their own writing pieces. For example, if students write a monologue from a historical figure's point of view, they can improvise a scene inspired by it.

6–8

Students can explore the alternative plans and major compromises considered by delegates at the Constitutional Convention. Ask them to consider events and people in history by enacting dramatic scenes that allow them to explore the question *What if?* What if a compromise were or were not reached? What if events had unfolded differently? Challenge students to give the subject different motivations and to change circumstances in the text to see how the event may have unfolded differently. This subtle shift requires students to remain true to their portrayal of a subject, but what fuels character choices will have dramatic implications on how the scene unfolds.

Name _____ Date _____

Drama Planner

Directions: Use the chart to help you plan your scene.

What story moment will you enact?

What characters will be involved in the scene?

What conflict or tension will trigger action in the scene?

What does each character want in the scene?

What action takes place in the scene?

What dialogue takes place in the scene?

Name _____ Date _____

Reading Reflection

Directions: As you prepare to enact the scene, you should use one or more of the following reading strategies. Check off the strategies as you use them.

Reading Strategies

❏ I reread to remember or to answer a question I had.

❏ I scanned for important information.

❏ I visualized the characters coming to life and the details of the setting.

❏ I thought about the problem and solution.

❏ I determined the author's message.

❏ I thought about what I already knew about the story.

Other strategies: _____

_____

Which strategy helped you most? Why? _____

_____

_____

_____

_____

_____

_____

Monologue

Model Lesson: Interpreting a Historical Figure

Model Lesson Overview

In this strategy, students learn about significant people who affected history and discover the importance of considering more than one historical source and perspective. Students compare information and think about different views, including biases. When possible, students inform their thinking for the monologue by reading direct quotations, diary entries, speeches, and letters from the historical figure in addition to sources written by those who knew the person and by those who studied him or her. Speaking directly to the audience as the historical figure, students reveal a conflict, a choice to be made, or a problem to be solved.

Standards

K–2

- Understands the contributions and significance of historical figures of the community
- Uses different voice level, phrasing, and intonation for different situations
- Creates and acts out the roles of characters from familiar stories

3–5

- Understands how the ideas of significant people affected the history of the state
- Uses variations of locomotor and nonlocomotor movement and vocal pitch, tempo, and tone for different characters
- Assumes roles that exhibit concentration and contribute to the action of dramatizations based on personal experience and heritage, imagination, literature, and history

6–8

- Understands that specific individuals and the values those individuals held had an impact on history
- Knows different types of primary and secondary sources and the motives, interests, and bias expressed in them (e.g., eyewitness accounts, letters, diaries, artifacts, photos; magazine articles, newspaper accounts, hearsay)
- Interacts as an invented character in improvised and scripted scenes
- Uses basic acting skills to develop characterizations that suggest artistic choices

Monologue *(cont.)*

Materials

- A collection of a variety of texts and primary and secondary sources about your chosen historical figure

- *Sample Monologue: Rachel Carson* (page 83, monorachelcarson.pdf)

- *Affecting History* (page 82, affectinghistory.pdf)

- *Monologue Planner* (page 84, monologueplanner.pdf)

Preparation

Choose several historical figures for students to learn about in more depth. Gather a collection of texts about the historical figures, such as biographies, historical fiction, poetry, articles, and primary and secondary sources. Many of these are available on the Library of Congress website. Historical figures may include those individuals significant to the history of our democracy (e.g., George Washington, Thomas Jefferson, Abraham Lincoln) and people over the last 200 years who have struggled to bring the liberties and equality promised in the basic principles of American democracy to all groups in American society (e.g., Sojourner Truth, Harriet Tubman, Frederick Douglass, W. E. B. Du Bois, Booker T. Washington, Susan B. Anthony, Martin Luther King, Jr., Rosa Parks, César Chávez).

Practice reading *Sample Monologue: Rachel Carson* (page 83) aloud, or select an example of a monologue from literature to share. You may find resources such as *Magnificent Monologues for Kids 2: More Kids' Monologues for Every Occasion!* by Chambers Stevens and *Minute Monologues for Kids* by Ruth Mae Roddy to be helpful. Additional ideas are provided in the Specific Grade Level Ideas.

Procedure

1. Distribute the *Affecting History* (page 82) activity sheet to students and explain that they will be researching a historical figure by using multiple sources and considering different perspectives. Assign or have students select a historical figure, and then have them complete the *Affecting History* activity sheet. Provide students with access to the collection of texts you gathered to aid them as they work. Allow time for them to research and record their findings.

2. Tell students that they will present the information they learned through monologue. If students are not familiar with what a monologue is, share examples. Talk with students about how a monologue is different from a dialogue.

Monologue *(cont.)*

3. Read the *Sample Monologue: Rachel Carson* (page 83) activity sheet (or your chosen monologue) to students *without* dramatic flair. Then, reread the monologue, asking students to close their eyes and visualize the character. How might the character look, talk, move, or behave? Ask students for suggestions on how you could read the monologue dramatically. For example, when could you change your voice, make a gesture, move, pause, or otherwise dramatize the reading? Model these ideas in another reading of the monologue. Discuss what students were able to learn about the character through the monologue and the way it was presented.

4. Group students together who have chosen or been assigned the same historical figure. Distribute the *Monologue Planner* (page 84) activity sheet to students and have group members work together to complete the *Monologue Planner* activity sheet.

5. After sufficient time, have students read over their group's list of ideas and think about which ideas suggest a conflict, which ideas could lead to effective dramatization, and which ideas suggest humor or emotion. Have students share their thinking with their group members and discuss possible ideas for a monologue.

6. Provide time for students to develop and rehearse individual monologues in class. Ask students to think about how to portray their historical figure with respect and dignity by avoiding stereotypical portrayals; giving attention to language, speaking patterns, and character traits; and honoring the complexity of real people in an authentic way.

7. Have students present their monologues. Debrief the experience, using the Questions for Discussion.

Questions for Discussion

- What insights did you gain into the historical figure?

- Where did you see character traits come through in the monologue?

- What was the character wrestling with?

- What emotions did you feel as you experienced the monologue?

- What challenges are there in representing someone who is different from you (language, cultural background, traditions, etc.)?

- In what ways did the character stay true to his or her ideals in the monologue?

- What sources were helpful? What biases did you discover?

Monologue *(cont.)*

Specific Grade Level Ideas

K–2

At this level, the activity can be improvisational. Give students a specific context to help them consider how their character would react in that situation. Assign students a historical figure whom they have prior knowledge of and ask them to imagine that they are entering a party where nobody knows them. How would they introduce themselves as the historical figure? What is important about how they look or where they can be found? The students can begin their monologues by saying, "Hi, I'm (name of character). Let me tell you a bit about myself." Ask students to imagine that the historical figure has something important on his or her mind and then express it in character.

3–5

Some students may wish to put on a show for invited guests. Help them practice performing their monologues. Allow students to write their monologues on index cards so that memorizing the lines does not become more important than the exploration of character. Once students become deeply familiar with a character by rehearsing their monologue, they will be able to accurately improvise the piece. Having the index cards available may help the performers relax as they share their work.

Students can explore through monologue the ways in which people have advanced the cause of human rights, equality, and the common good, such as the work of Clara Barton or Jackie Robinson. Monologue is a powerful way to explore people who have worked to advance animal rights as well, such as Jane Goodall.

Monologue *(cont.)*

6–8

Students can explore the differences between leaders such as George Washington, Alexander Hamilton, and Thomas Jefferson, and they can explore the social and economic composition of each political party in the 1790s. Students should also discuss the contradictions that might be presented among multiple sources. It is important for students to explore contradictions in character traits as they learn from different perspectives. For example, students may wrestle with Thomas Jefferson's character traits as the primary author of the Declaration of Independence, father of his enslaved children with Sally Hemings, father of his white children, and slave master. Have students create monologues from the point of view of those whose voices have been traditionally left out, such as a monologue for one of Thomas Jefferson's enslaved children. Consider having students read the historical fiction text *Jefferson's Sons* by Kimberly Brubaker Bradley.

Name _____ Date _____

Affecting History

Directions: Use the chart to explore how a historical figure affected history and the sources of information about the figure.

Historical figure: _____

How does this compare to information from other sources? / How does this compare to what you already know?			
Describe the historical figure's character traits, his or her ideas that affected history, what actions he or she took, and other important information.			
Describe the source of information (e.g., newspaper account, photograph, or magazine article).			

 #51092—*Strategies to Integrate the Arts in Social Studies*

Sample Monologue: Rachel Carson

(Rachel Carson is speaking on the telephone.)

Hello, may I speak with Jane, please? This is Rachel Carson, the author of *Silent Spring*. Jane asked if I would be willing to come and speak about my book. Yes, of course I'll hold.

(waits briefly)

Hi, Jane. I received your invitation and...well, thank you. I have to say, though, I am a bit hesitant to speak. I see myself much more as a writer than I do a speaker, actually. And it's just that—I'm a biologist and not accustomed to speaking to large groups. I'm just trying to uncover the truth about what pesticides are doing—they're poisonous and people need to hear it.

I've worked at the U.S. Bureau of Fisheries, and I have seen firsthand what chemicals like DDT can do. These poisons get into shrimp and fish and birds, and they travel through the food chain.

It's not that I'm opposed to the use of pesticides altogether—it's that they are used so freely, without thought to the lasting effects. People need to know the facts and decide for themselves.

The good news is that people are starting to take action. In fact, I just heard that President Kennedy has asked the President's Science Advisory Committee to conduct an investigation to consider the effects on the environment and human life, and this could lead to some new legislation. My book has really raised a ruckus, and I'm really glad to see it! Some folks in Maine just voted to cancel aerial spraying of their beautiful island. Change is happening, so it's important to get the word out. People have to know.

I just...well...I guess I should get up there and talk to them myself and make the case in the most compelling way I can—for all living things...and for the Earth. We are just a tiny part of a vast and incredible universe.

So...yes, I will come and speak. Let me get a pen, and I'll get the information about when and where.

Name _____ Date _____

Monologue Planner

Directions: Answer the questions to help plan your monologue.

What character traits does the character show? How?	How old is your character? Where does he or she live? What does he or she like and dislike?
What historical details will you include?	What challenge, decision, or dilemma does the character face?
What is the character trying to reveal?	How does the character feel? What facial expressions and body stances portray this feeling?
How will your voice change to reflect emotion and character?	What will the character realize at the end of the monologue?

Improvisation

Model Lesson: Economics in Action

Model Lesson Overview

In this strategy, students apply their understanding of economics as they improvise a dramatic historical scene. Students work from a picture book about scarcity of resources, or they improvise a scene from a newspaper article or the media that depicts a current event about the scarcity of resources and wants of individuals, governments, or societies. As students improvise scenes, they experience choices and opportunity costs. Circumstances and character motivation come together to influence how a scene progresses.

Standards

K–2

- Understands that since people cannot have everything they want, they must make choices about using goods and services to satisfy wants

- Knows that people who use goods and services are called consumers, and people who make goods or provide services are called producers, and that most people both produce and consume

- Plans and prepares improvisations

3–5

- Understands that choices usually involve trade-offs; people can give up buying or doing a little of one thing in order to buy or do a little of something else

- Understands that goods and services are scarce because there are not enough productive resources to satisfy all of the wants of individuals, governments, and societies

- Provides rationales for personal preferences about the whole as well as the parts of dramatic performances

6–8

- Understands that scarcity of resources necessitates choice at both the personal and the societal levels

- Understands that the evaluation of choices and opportunity costs is subjective and differs across individuals and societies

- Uses basic acting skills to develop characterizations that suggest artistic choices

Improvisation *(cont.)*

Materials

- Text, picture book, media clip, newspaper article, or other source about scarcity of resources, opportunity cost, and choice

- *Getting Ready for Improvisation* (page 89, improvisation.pdf)

Preparation

Decide whether the scenes will be about economics in a present-day context or in a historical context, and gather books, articles, and media clips accordingly. Consider material that will inspire scenes and allow students to improvise decision making based on wants and costs. The book *The Great Kapok Tree: A Tale of the Amazon Rain Forest* by Lynne Cherry is a good resource. Decide if you will to give students a choice in their reading and viewing of materials or if the class will improvise scenes from the same source.

In the days and weeks prior to the lesson, have students keep an ongoing list of vocabulary words such as *wants*, *needs*, *goods*, *services*, *resources*, *consumer*, *consumption cost*, *benefit*, *natural resources*, *human resources*, and *capital resources*. Additional ideas are provided in the Specific Grade Level Ideas.

Procedure

1. Share a picture book, a text, a newspaper article, a media clip, or another selection with students to use to demonstrate the strategy. Discuss the economic ideas of scarcity of resources, choices, and opportunity costs as shown in the material, and review the vocabulary lists that students have compiled.

2. Tell students that they will be using improvisation to create a scene based on their reading or based on an original idea about economic decision making. Choose a scene from the resource you shared, and have a student volunteer help you model the use of improvisation to act out the scene. Model what a subject may be thinking or saying by using words that come to mind based on the ideas and motivations associated with the decision making. For example, in *The Great Kapok Tree: A Tale of the Amazon Rain Forest*, a young man is asked to cut down a large kapok tree in the Amazon to clear space for planting but considers the needs of people in contrast to the needs of the animals. A scene could be created that explores environmental conservation and issues of scarcity by having the young man work to persuade his boss to see the impact of cutting down trees on the environment and the animals that live in the rain forest.

Improvisation *(cont.)*

3. Distribute the *Getting Ready for Improvisation* (page 89) activity sheet to students and additional books, articles, and resources about the topic. Have students work in small groups or pairs to choose a scene from one of the sources or create their own original scene. Have students use the activity sheet to plan their improvisation. Remind students that they do not need to plan the dialogue, just the general progression of the scene. They will improvise the words that the characters say. Use the Planning Questions to guide students as they plan their scenes.

4. Invite students to share their improvisations with the whole class. Discuss the scenes, using the Questions for Discussion.

Planning Questions

- Where does the event take place?

- What is happening?

- What do you know about the subjects?

- What might the subject be saying?

- What dilemma do the characters have related to scarcity that will create dramatic tension and interest?

- How might you bring the scene to life in words and movement?

- How might you create your scene with a clear beginning, middle, and end?

Questions for Discussion

- What choices were made that brought the scene to life?

- What character traits were demonstrated through the improvisation?

- How did improvisation help you better understand the scarcity of resources and the choices involved?

- What did the improvisation tell you about economics that the reading or viewing did not?

Improvisation *(cont.)*

Specific Grade Level Ideas

K–2

Students can focus their improvisations on the concept of bartering by making decisions in the moment to trade goods and services for other goods and services without using money. Viewers of the improvisation can discuss how two people trade because they want to and that they expect to be better off after the exchange.

3–5

As an extension, invite students to create scenes that were not in the reading or viewing material. Ask them to create new characters and consider what characters or circumstances would shift the way that the events unfold and enact a variety of options. Once complete, they can document their improvisations in writing, noting the back-and-forth dialogue and description of action.

6–8

Have students use improvisation to create a debate scenario. Provide students with questions or controversial issues, and then ask them to improvise and defend one side or the other of the historical or present-day argument. Students can also use improvisation to create a conversation between two historical figures.

Name _____ Date _____

Getting Ready for Improvisation

Directions: Work with your partner or group to choose one of the following options and write ideas for action or dialogue for your characters. Create a sketch or diagram to map out how your character will move through the scene.

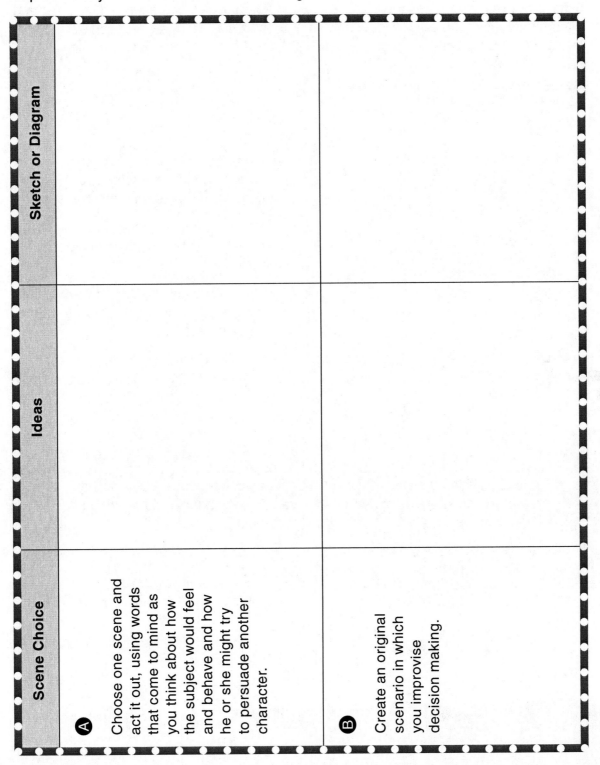

Sketch or Diagram		
Ideas		
Scene Choice	Ⓐ Choose one scene and act it out, using words that come to mind as you think about how the subject would feel and behave and how he or she might try to persuade another character.	Ⓑ Create an original scenario in which you improvise decision making.

Scriptwriting

Model Lesson: Scenes Reveal Culture

Model Lesson Overview

In this strategy, students choose an excerpt from a book about a topic of study and write their own script to tell the story. They consider setting, character motivations, and dialogue as they tell stories about cultures of the world—their historical achievements, family life, ceremonies, and more.

Standards

K–2

- Knows the basic components of culture

- Engages in fantasy dramatic play

- Selects interrelated characters, environments, and situations for simple dramatizations

3–5

- Understands various aspects of family life, structures, and roles in different cultures and in many eras

- Knows significant historical achievements of various cultures of the world

- Knows characters in dramatizations, their relationships, and their environments

- Knows how visual elements (e.g., space, color, line, shape, texture) and aural aspects are used to communicate locale and mood

6–8

- Understands the general relationship between cultural perspectives and practices (e.g., holidays, celebrations, work habits, play) in the target and native cultures

- Creates characters, environments (e.g., place, time, atmosphere/mood), and actions that create tension and suspense

Materials

- Text or texts about a world culture

- *Script Ideas* (pages 94–95, scriptideas.pdf)

- *Observation Record* (page 96, observationrecord.pdf)

Scriptwriting *(cont.)*

Preparation

Decide what text or texts about culture you will have students use, according to your chosen topic of study. Determine whether small groups will draw excerpts from the same text or from a choice of texts. Additional ideas are provided in the Specific Grade Level Ideas.

Procedure

1. Ask students to share the different experiences they have had with viewing or acting in plays. Ask students, "What is a scene?" Talk about how scenes in a play are similar to chapters of a book. Discuss what a script is and how it is formatted.

2. Share your chosen text or texts with students. Discuss the aspects of culture that are revealed in the text (e.g., holidays, traditions, and/or family structures). Tell students that they will choose an excerpt from the text and tell the story by writing a script that highlights aspects of culture. Tell students that they will then stage a dramatic reading of their script (a reading of the script in character but without staging or movement). Students should focus on bringing the story to life using character voice and inflection.

3. Have students select an excerpt from the chosen text or texts to investigate through scriptwriting. Divide students into small groups according to the scene they have chosen. Distribute the *Script Ideas* (pages 94–95) activity sheet to groups and have them complete the handout. Use the Planning Questions to guide students' planning process.

4. Allow time for groups to write their scripts and practice dramatic reading, including volume, pacing, fluency, emotion, and expression.

5. Have groups perform a dramatic reading of their scripts for the class while the audience members complete the *Observation Record* (page 96) activity sheet.

6. Debrief using the Questions for Discussion.

Planning Questions

- What excerpt from the text will you choose to turn into a script? Why?

- What conversations or dialogue will take place?

- How many scenes will your script be divided into?

- Who are the characters? What are their thoughts, feelings, and motivations?

- Will you use a narrator to set the scene and bridge material?

Scriptwriting (cont.)

Questions for Discussion

- How is a script different from text in a book?

- How does the story you told through scriptwriting compare to the story told in the text excerpt?

- How did a dramatic reading help tell the story?

- How did the dialogue between characters illuminate particular aspects of the story?

- What role did the narrator play? Was he or she a character? Was he or she a voice external to the story?

- How did the scenes work together to tell a story?

Specific Grade Level Ideas

K–2

It is important to show students examples of scripts and the visual format of a script. Point out the amount of blank space in a script compared to the text in a book. Show students how to write the character's name followed by what they say (dialogue). Provide students with a simple model.

Gather a group of books about holidays and ceremonies of different cultures and read the texts so that they become familiar for students. Have groups choose one of the books from the collection and write a script for an exciting part of the book.

Students can also use scriptwriting to explore how a *legend* is a story that comes down from the past or how a *myth* is a traditional story that often explains cultural practices or beliefs.

3–5

Have students re-create a scene from a historical play they have viewed at school or online and write their own script to tell the story. Then, have students compare and contrast the different versions.

Share primary source photographs with students and invite them to write a script for the events and people in the photographs. Students can also use scriptwriting to explore the origin of the names of places, rivers, cities, and counties and the various cultural influences within a region.

Scriptwriting *(cont.)*

6–8

Invite students to read poetry as an inspiration for scriptwriting. For example, have students consider the literary works of the central leaders of Transcendentalism. They can also write scripts based on information gleaned from historical documents, diary entries, and video and audio clips.

Name _____ Date _____

Script Ideas

Directions: Complete the chart to help you form ideas for writing a script.

Elements of the Scene	Script Ideas
Describe the setting.	
Describe the characters: • names • traits • motivations	
List important conversations or dialogue.	

Name _____ Date _____

Script Ideas *(cont.)*

Elements of the Scene	Script Ideas
Describe aspects of culture to reveal: • traditions, holidays, ceremonies • family life, structures, or roles • historical achievements	
How will you use the role of narrator to set the stage, add important external commentary, and help bridge scene changes?	

Name _____ Date _____

Observation Record

Directions: As you listen to and watch the dramatic script readings, use the chart to record the dramatic choices and important social studies ideas.

Classmate and Title of Script	Dramatic Choice Observations	Important Social Studies Ideas

Music

Music

Understanding Music

Music has played a significant role in every culture since the beginning of time. Due to recent technology, our favorite tunes are readily available to us, and music has become even more prevalent in our lives. Dr. Howard Gardner has identified musical intelligence as one form of intelligence (2011). His theory of multiple intelligences suggests that students learn in different ways, and for some students, connecting with rhythm, beat, and melody provides access to learning. And as any adult who has introduced a cleanup song knows, music can motivate children and help them make transitions from one activity to another. Recently, attention has been given to the benefits of music in academic performance. It has been suggested that early music training develops language skills, spatial relations, and memory (Perret and Fox 2006). Kelli Paquette and Sue Rieg also note that incorporating music into the early childhood classroom is particularly beneficial to English language learners' literacy development (2008).

Gayla Kolb explores the natural relationship between music and literacy, noting that "the spontaneous disposition children have toward rhythm and melody makes music an ideal tool for assisting them with interwoven facets of language: listening, speaking, reading, and writing. Through music, children experience the wholeness of language" (1996).

In the strategies for this section, students explore a variety of historical writing and social studies concepts through the integration of music and sound. Students engage in singing, playing, composing, and conducting the music in the context of exploring historical characters, time lines, and settings. No previous musical training is needed for you or your students.

Bill Harp notes, "Music and reading go together because singing is a celebration of language." Because our language has natural rhythms and melody, "children bring this natural 'music' language with them to the task of learning to read, and so using singing to teach reading draws on this natural understanding" (1988, 454). The more avenues we provide for students to experience and explore the patterns of language, the more likely we are to connect with the variable ways in which students learn.

Strategies for Music

∞) Found Sounds

Sounds are all around us; they are found when we attend to them or manipulate them. Think about the sound of light rain or the squeals of delight you hear near a playground. There is rhythm in these sounds. Composer R. Murray Schafer thinks about the world as a musical composition. He notes, "In [music] we try to get people to use their senses to listen carefully, to look carefully" (quoted in New 2009). What makes a sound music rather than noise may depend on the listener, but it is also related to pitch (high or low) and rhythm. When students collect found sounds, they gain a new appreciation for what music is and develop careful listening skills. They can also better understand the environment from which sounds come. Students can put sounds together in interesting compositions, exploring environment and contexts for where history has unfolded as well as the power of onomatopoeia as language mirroring sounds. Louise Pascale notes, "Often, we describe things visually rather than auditorially. Students can describe the sounds they find in a vivid way (e.g., a *loud* sound can become an *ear-piercing sound, brassy, shattering,* etc.). This can build language" (Pascale, pers. comm. 2012).

∞) Songwriting

When students sing, a deep connection is created with the melody, rhythm, and lyrics of a song. Further, creating and making music supports academic achievement (Deasy 2002). Though students have opportunities to sing in school, far less attention is given to their ability to create their own songs. This strategy invites students to become songwriters, and as they do so, they become more familiar with the importance of tone, rhythm, and beat. Students can begin on an intuitive level or simplify the task, for example, by creating new lyrics for a song they already know. As songs can help us remember things, these adaptations can help students retain information from a variety of social studies texts. Also, writing lyrics will prompt students to discuss, synthesize, and categorize curricular concepts. Students can explore rhythms on a drum or experiment with notes on a keyboard. As their musical knowledge expands, they can create and perform original melodies.

Music *(cont.)*

✆ Chants

Chants involve the rhythmic repetition of sounds or words. They can be sung or spoken. They can be a component of spiritual practices or heard on a football field. By combining different dynamics (ranging from soft to loud), pitch (variations from high to low), and different notes (length of duration), students can create engaging sound effects that help them learn and remember ideas. According to Sonja Dunn (1999), "a chant is a rhythmic group recitation." Chants can be used in a variety of ways. They can be created with catchy rhythms that make the associated words easy to learn and to remember. When this form of chant is emphasized, students retain important information. Chants also can be constructed by layering phrases on top of each other that are then spoken or sung simultaneously. In this format, the use of differing rhythms and pitch create interest and suggest relationships among the chosen phrases and thus the content being considered. Chants allow for the exploration and observation of the natural rhythms of language.

✆ Soundscapes

In this strategy, students create a sense of setting through the layering of sound effects. Students "analyze a particular event or situation purely through sound, and then re-create it. The audience listens to the performance with eyes closed while the performers, if successful, bring the environment immediately and accurately alive through sound alone. The audience will feel as if they are immersed in the soundscape, whether it is the rainforest, a desert oasis, a moment in the Civil War, Napoleon's March, or a moment in time from a chapter book the class is reading. The challenge for the performers is to carefully select just the essential sounds and place them sequentially in such a way that produces an accurate reproduction of the sound environment" (Donovan and Pascale 2012).

✆ Mash-Up

Creating mash-ups involves assembling parts from a variety of songs or music to create a new composition. Drawing from a range of ideas and piecing together already existing musical ideas, new innovations can be developed. Students create mash-ups by combining the lyrics from two songs from historical time periods and discovering how music can be connected with historical moments and relationships throughout history.

Found Sounds

Model Lesson: Industrialization

Model Lesson Overview

Students explore industrialization through found sounds. After exploring various primary and secondary sources, such as listening to audio files and video clips or viewing photographs of the Industrial Revolution, students re-create the sounds with found objects in the classroom, school, environment, or at home in order to represent the ideas and technologies of industrialization. Partners play their musical "found sounds" for others and listen to the presentations of their peers.

Standards

K–2

- Understands major discoveries in science and technology, some of their social and economic effects, and the major scientists and inventors responsible for them

- Uses a variety of sound sources when composing

3–5

- Understands the impact of the factory system on the daily life of children

- Performs simple pieces with appropriate dynamics

- Performs simple pieces in rhythm

6–8

- Understands the effect of the Industrial Revolution on social and political conditions in various regions

- Uses a variety of nontraditional sound sources when composing and arranging

- Performs with expression and technical accuracy on a string, wind, percussion, or other classroom instrument

9–12

- Understands the impact of the Industrial Revolution during the early and later 19th century

- Uses the elements of music for expressive effect

Materials

- Audio files or video clips about the Industrial Revolution

- Variety of objects in classroom or environment to use to create sounds

- *Found Sounds* (page 106, foundsounds.pdf)

Found Sounds *(cont.)*

Preparation

In the days and weeks prior to this lesson, have students study the Industrial Revolution. Locate primary sources such as photographs in addition to secondary sources such as resources from the Library of Congress website. Audio files and video clips allow students to hear the sounds of the time period. Also, gather objects to demonstrate the idea of a found sound, such as paper to be crunched, the repeated tapping of a ruler, a pencil hitting a wastebasket, or the slow turning of a pencil sharpener. Additional ideas are provided in the Specific Grade Level Ideas.

Procedure

1. Activate students' prior knowledge with questions about the concept of study. Ask students, "What was daily life like for children in the factories? What were the machines of the New England mill towns like in the early 1800s?"

2. Tell students that they will use found sounds to represent the ideas and inventions of the Industrial Revolution. Demonstrate the idea of a found sound by using objects you collected, such as striking kitchen utensils or crunching tinfoil.

3. Play audio or video clips related to the historical period, and have students listen carefully to the sounds they hear. Ask for a student volunteer to choose a sound from the clip for the class to re-create with found sounds. Ask the class for ideas about objects that could re-create this sound.

4. Divide students into pairs and distribute the *Found Sounds* (page 106) activity sheet to partners. If possible, distribute copies of primary source photographs related to the topic of study. Direct students to select three ideas or technologies from the Industrial Revolution and use found sounds to represent them.

5. Allow time for students to try making found sounds with different objects and combinations of objects. As partners work, use the Planning Questions to stimulate students' thinking. Encourage students to create more than one found sound and link them together in a composition.

6. Have students share their found sounds with the class.

7. Debrief the class, using the Questions for Discussion.

Planning Questions

- What are some objects in the classroom that you might use to create sounds?

- Will you play sounds separately or together?

- How will you consider rhythm and tempo?

- How might you combine sounds?

Found Sounds *(cont.)*

Questions for Discussion

- In what ways did re-creating sounds help you understand the event or time period?

- In what ways did re-creating the sounds help you understand the impact of the event on the people?

- How did you decide which sounds would be played together?

- What did you notice from hearing the found sounds of others?

Specific Grade Level Ideas

K–2

As a pre-lesson or follow-up activity, take students outside to listen for sounds. The sound outing could be to the cafeteria or to the playground. Have students bring along notebooks and list words that come to mind as they hear the sounds. Discuss ways to re-create the sounds they observe.

Students can investigate the tools and technology of the Industrial Revolution through found sounds. Gather primary source photographs and video clips to show students the inventions of the time period and have them re-create the sounds from the clips with found sounds. Students can also explore the similarities and differences between where products are made in urban areas compared to suburban areas. Extend the lesson to today's manufacturing.

Students could use found sounds to represent ideas from other times and places in history, such as a colonial community, a pioneer farming community, or various immigrant communities, or to show changes in family and school life over time.

3–5

Students can collect found sounds to understand how the character and function of cities have changed over time. Invite students to collect found sounds at home and bring them into class. Have students take turns playing their found sounds for the class. Ask the class to listen with their eyes closed to keep the source of the sound a secret. After hearing the found sound, have students write to explore what the sounds remind them of, who or what would make these sounds, and what images come to mind when hearing the sounds. Then, reveal the source of the found sound.

Found Sounds *(cont.)*

6–8

Students can use found sounds to explore the impact of the Industrial Revolution in the 18th-century Atlantic Basin, in 18th-century Europe, or in 18th-century England. Have them collect objects to create found sounds that will enhance their understanding of the technologies, hardships, and atmosphere of the time.

Students can also create a composition using their found sounds. In order to create a composition, ask students to think about the timing of who will play which found sound at a given time. Will they play all at once, or take turns? Will the found sounds overlap? Invite students to perform their composition for the class.

Students could use found sounds to represent or interpret various historical eras, events, and themes such as the rise and fall of various civilizations, global expansion, or historical moments such as the Boston Tea Party.

9–12

Have students explore the various innovations of the Industrial Revolution by using found sounds to capture the essence of inventions and technological advancements of the time period. For example, have students create compositions that mirror the sounds laborers—including children—may have heard in a textile factory, an assembly line, or other locations where workers were placed in often dangerous and crowded areas to produce goods in mass quantities. Students can compose pieces that communicate these harsh conditions, using found sounds that are cacophonic in nature and similarly express the harsh nature of the working conditions.

As an extension, have students pretend they are muckrakers during the Industrial Revolution and have them write investigative journal pieces to be read alongside their musical compositions. Students can also use found sounds to communicate concepts related to other innovations, such as glassmaking, canals, roads, railways, steam power, the cotton gin, patents, labor unions, and the many riots that resulted from the working conditions of the Industrial Revolution.

Name _____ Date _____

Found Sounds

Directions: Use the chart to help you use found sounds to represent ideas and events in a particular time.

Found Sound	What idea or event will you represent?	How will you create your found sound?	How does your found sound enhance your understanding of the idea or event?
1			
2			
3			

Songwriting

Model Lesson: Immigration

Model Lesson Overview

In this strategy, students use songwriting to explore the causes and experiences of immigration. As a scaffold, students become familiar with the melody and lyrics of an original song by David Williams about the causes of Irish immigration to the United States in 1845 and the immigrants' experiences. They use this song as a form of mentor text to write their own lyrics about immigration. An instrumental version of the song is available on the Digital Resource CD so students can sing their original lyrics to the melody in addition to the mentor lyrics.

Standards

K-2

- Knows that different groups immigrated to the state or region

- Understands how people have helped newcomers get settled and learn the ways of the new country (e.g., family members, fraternal organizations, houses of worship)

- Sings invented songs

3-5

- Knows the origins of various groups who immigrated to the United States

- Knows why various immigrant groups left their countries of origin

- Sings ostinatos, partner songs, and rounds

- Improvises simple rhythmic variations and simple melodic embellishments on familiar melodies

6-8

- Understands the motivations of European migrants and immigrants in the 19th century

- Understands trends in immigration out of Europe in the 19th century

- Improvises short melodies, unaccompanied and over given rhythmic accompaniments, in a consistent style

- Knows music that represents diverse genres and cultures

Songwriting *(cont.)*

Materials

- Immigration primary sources

- *Famine Song, Grades K–5* (page 113, famineK–5.pdf) or
  Famine Song, Grades 6–12 (page 114, famine6–12.pdf)

- Audio recording: "Famine Song, Grades K–5" (famineK–5.mp3) or
  "Famine Song, Grades 6–12" (famine6–12.mp3)

- Audio recording: "Famine Song" Instrumental Version
  (famineinstrumental.mp3)

- *Lyric Brainstorming Guide* (page 111, lyricbrainstorming.pdf)

- *Songwriting Planner* (page 112, songwritingplanner.pdf)

Preparation

In the days and weeks prior to the lesson, have students study immigration, providing them with the opportunity to view primary sources such as those available on the Library of Congress website. Determine if students will write song lyrics with partners or individually. Listen to "Famine Song, Grades K–5" (famineK–5.mp3) or "Famine Song, Grades 6–12" (famine6–12.mp3), whichever is most appropriate for your students, and decide which version to play. Additional ideas are provided in the Specific Grade Level Ideas.

Procedure

1. Ask questions to activate students' prior knowledge about immigration, such as, "What is an immigrant? Why did different immigrant groups leave their countries of origin?" Share the primary sources you collected to deepen students' connection to concepts related to immigration.

2. Define musical terms that you will be referencing throughout the lesson, such as *melody* (the tune of a song), *lyrics* (the words of a song), and *chorus* (the repeating lines of a song).

3. Distribute *Famine Song, Grades K–5* (page 113) or *Famine Song, Grades 6–12* (page 114), whichever is most appropriate for your students. Then, play either "Famine Song, Grades K–5" (famineK–5.mp3) or "Famine Song, Grades 6–12" (famine6–12.mp3), depending on where your students are developmentally, and have the class follow along with the lyrics.

4. Discuss how the song tells the story of an immigrant group. Have students locate details that describe the causes and experiences of immigration in the song. Discuss how the chorus reveals the main idea and the verses provide details.

Songwriting *(cont.)*

5. Give students multiple opportunities to sing along and become familiar with the melody.

6. Ask students to choose an immigrant group about which to write their own lyrics, using the melody from the instrumental version of "Famine Song" (famineinstrumental.mp3). Use the Planning Questions to stimulate students' thinking.

7. Have students complete the *Lyric Brainstorming Guide* (page 111) activity sheet to develop potential rhymes for their lyrics by brainstorming words that may rhyme with the word ending each line.

8. Have students complete the *Songwriting Planner* (page 112) activity sheet, writing original lyrics for the chorus and one verse using the "Famine Song" melody.

9. Allow students to share their songs with the class as you play the instrumental version of "Famine Song," having them sing their original lyrics.

10. Use the Questions for Discussion to talk about the process of songwriting to deepen their understanding of immigration.

Planning Questions

- Will you write original lyrics to a verse, a chorus, or an entire song?

- What important ideas will you include in the chorus?

- What details will you include in the verse?

Questions for Discussion

- How did you decide what information to include in your lyrics?

- What were the challenges of songwriting?

- How did songwriting help you understand the causes and experiences of immigration?

- What did you learn about immigration from listening to others' songs?

Songwriting *(cont.)*

Specific Grade Level Ideas

K–2

As you read books aloud, view videos, and examine primary sources such as maps, prints, photographs, diaries, and letters about immigrant groups, record information for potential lyrics on a class chart. Then, work together to write a chorus for a class song that tells about the immigrant groups. Encourage students to create a chorus of their own. You may also write lyrics of your own that help students understand the emotions of leaving family behind, the significance of preserving cultural traditions, and how people helped newcomers get settled and learn the ways of the new country (e.g., family members, fraternal organizations, houses of worship).

Students can also write songs about how democratic values came to be or how important figures reacted to their times and why they were significant. They could also interpret the meaning of legends and myths and write the ideas through song.

3–5

In addition to the K–2 Specific Grade Level Ideas, challenge students to write additional verses. Have students include a verse that shows how they understand the obstacles and opportunities an immigrant group encountered when they arrived in the United States. Students can also explore through songwriting the forced relocation of American Indians and how their lives, rights, and territories were affected by European colonization and expansion of the United States.

6–8

Students can use the melody of "Famine Song" and write original lyrics about an immigrant group of study. You could also challenge them to create their own melody. Have students explore the connection between industrialization and immigration. Provide opportunities for students to research primary and secondary sources on websites such as the Library of Congress and PBS's Destination America. Students can also use songwriting to explore resistance movements of different groups over time.

Name _____ Date _____

Lyric Brainstorming Guide

Directions: Complete the chart to help you write meaningful song lyrics.

Immigrant group and country of origin:	
Causes of immigration:	Obstacles and opportunities in the new country:
Lyric ideas:	Potential rhymes:

Name _____ Date _____

Songwriting Planner

Directions: Write original lyrics to tell about an immigrant group. Then, use the checklist to help prepare for performing your song.

Immigrant Group: _____

Write lyrics for the **chorus**. Capture the important ideas.

_____

_____

_____

_____

Write lyrics for one **verse**.

_____

_____

_____

_____

Songwriting Checklist

❑ I know the melody to my song by heart.

❑ I used rhythm and/or rhyme.

❑ The words to my song go along with the beat.

Name _____   Date _____

Famine Song, Grades K–5

"Famine Song"
by David Williams

(Verse 1)

In the year of our Lord, eighteen forty and five,

When first this most terrible blight did arrive,

No one could know, we could not have foreseen

The fate of the good folk of poor Skibbereen.

When I think of that morn, my heart beats like a drum

The sight that foretold of the Hunger to come.

The family woke early to a dawn damp and still,

To a fog on the land, and the air unco' chill.

(Chorus)

Darkness, it fell o'er the fields of this land,

Turning the praties to dust in our hands.

I'll not stay in Ireland where there's fear all around—

On America's shores will my fortune be found.

(Verse 2)

We looked o'er the fields through the mist at first light.

Said Da, "Seems the harvest is lost to the blight.

Hard times are ahead, and we'd best face the truth:

Our hopes lie in you, now, and all Ireland's youth."

So our tickets arrived from my Aunt Mary Ann

To set sail for Boston as soon as I can.

And I dream all that night of a bright flag unfurled,

That flies o'er a country that welcomes the world.

(Repeat Chorus)

(Verse 3)

In the harbor at Cork, a ship can be seen,

For there lies at her anchor the Bark General Greene.

I'll board her and away from old Ireland I'll slip,

Just another poor soul on a dark sailing ship.

And I'll take my chances, like a million before

And cross the cold deep to America's shore,

Where Ma can find work, and I'll find my pride,

And at last my hope rises, along with the tide.

(Repeat Chorus × 2)

Printed with Permission: Title—"Early Tracks," including several songs, one of which is "Famine Song." Author/Copyright Claimant/Rights & Permissions—David George Alexander Williams, Registration # - SRu 1-082-776, Date—July 27, 2012

Name _____ Date _____

Famine Song, Grades 6–12

"Famine Song"
by David Williams

(Verse 1)

In the year of our Lord, eighteen forty and five,

When first this most terrible blight did arrive,

No one could know, we could not have foreseen

The fate of the good folk of poor Skibbereen.

I'll never forget it, long as I draw breath,

The sight that foretold of starvation and death.

The family woke early to a dawn damp and still,

To a fog on the land, and the air unco' chill.

(Chorus)

The Angel of Death spread her wings o'er this land,

Sowing the seeds of our doom with her hand.

I'll not stay in Ireland to be laid in the ground—

On America's shores will my fortune be found.

(Verse 2)

We surveyed the fields through the mist at first light.

Said Da, "Sure the devil's worked hard all this night.

He's taken our crops, which so lately were rich,

And work'd magic most foul to turn all black as pitch."

And now Ma's in the poorhouse, and Da's in the grave,

One is a corpse and the other a slave,

And which of them's better off, I could not say,

For Father's at rest, but Ma toils all the day.

(Repeat Chorus)

(Verse 3)

In the harbor at Cork, a ship can be seen,

For there lies at her anchor the Bark General Greene.

I'll board her and away from old Ireland we'll slip,

Just another poor soul on a foul coffin ship.

And I'll take my chances, like a million before,

That I make it alive to America's shore,

Where a man can find work, and perhaps find his pride

And at last my hope rises, along with the tide.

(Repeat Chorus × 2)

Printed with Permission: Title—"Early Tracks," including several songs, one of which is "Famine Song" Author/Copyright Claimant/Rights & Permissions—David George Alexander Williams, Registration # - SRu 1-082-776, Date—July 27, 2012

Chants

Model Lesson: Expression of Culture

Model Lesson Overview

In this lesson, students use chants to understand how stories and music are expressions of culture. Students read a variety of folktales from cultures they are studying, from various regions of the United States or from other countries. Then, students create their own chants to represent the story and culture.

Standards

K–2

- Understands that folktales reflect the beliefs of various cultures in the past
- Understands that music can reflect the daily life, history, and beliefs of a country
- Sings invented songs
- Sings simple, familiar songs

3–5

- Understands the folklore and other cultural contributions from various regions of the United States and how they helped to form a national heritage
- Improvises simple rhythmic variations and simple melodic embellishments on familiar melodies

6–8

- Knows that language, stories, folktales, music, and artistic creations are expressions of culture
- Improvises melodic embellishments and simple rhythmic and melodic variations

Materials

- Folktales from regions of the United States or other countries
- *Sample Chants* (page 118, chants.pdf)
- *Chant Planner* (page 119, chantplanner.pdf)

Preparation

Locate various folktales that represent regions of the United States or other countries. Select one folktale as a model. Additional ideas are provided in the Specific Grade Level Ideas.

Chants *(cont.)*

Procedure

1. Share your chosen folktale with students. Discuss the ways in which the folktale expresses the culture of a group, such as daily life, beliefs, history, food, or religion by locating evidence in the text. Record these details for students to reference throughout the lesson.

2. Explain to students that one way to remember facts, characteristics of a concept, or sequencing of ideas is through chants. Display the *Sample Chants* (page 118) activity sheet and lead students in reading them aloud. Explain that the first chant explores the traits of the Aztec deity Tezcatlipoca, the lord of the night. Tell students that this legend was passed down through generations through the oral tradition. Then, move on to the second chant, explaining that in this chant, Tezcatlipoca is calling on the wind gods to rescue musicians who are trapped by the sun, Tonatiuh. This chant highlights the moment when the wind encounters the sun and struggles to free the musicians so that color and music can return to Earth. Ask students to discuss the characteristics of the chants they hear and identify the aspects of culture they communicate.

3. Introduce students to the idea of *rhythm* (repeating beat), *dynamics* (softness or loudness of the voice), and *pitch* (high or low vocal tone). Divide the class into groups. Assign each group one of the lines of a sample chant to repeat together. Ask one group to repeat its line rhythmically, using low pitch, soft dynamics, and steady beat. Ask the next group to use medium pitch, medium dynamics, and steady beat. Ask the next group to use high pitch, high dynamics, and steady beat.

4. Tell students that they will create a chant to represent the meaning of the folktale and that they will decide when to use specific words and phrases from the tale and when to paraphrase. Have students complete the *Chant Planner* (page 119) activity sheet in small groups and create their chant. Use the Planning Questions to guide students' thinking.

5. Have each group perform their chant for the class. Debrief using the Questions for Discussion.

Planning Questions

- What pitch (high or low) will you use?

- How loud (dynamics) will you be?

- What other sound effects could you add to give your chant more interest (clapping, stomping, slapping the desk, and so forth)?

- Are there gestures you could add to emphasize your tempo (slow, curved motions or quick, jagged movements)?

Chants *(cont.)*

Questions for Discussion

- How does your chant express the culture of a group?

- Which words or phrases did you choose and why?

- How did you decide when to paraphrase and when to quote directly from the tale?

- How did the rhythm of the lines work when the lines were layered?

- How did different pitch, dynamics, and rhythm affect the way lines sounded together?

- What other ideas could you experiment with to make your chant more interesting?

Specific Grade Level Ideas

K–2

Have students create the chant as a class and then add an additional part on their own. Students can also explore through chanting the different sectors that are part of community life, what natural resources are in the area, or traditions that belong to specific cultures.

3–5

As an extension, divide students into small groups and invite them to create a chant for another folktale. Students can also explore the folklore from different regions of the United States and represent how they helped form a national heritage, naming the regions of the United States and their characteristics. Students can also create chants about trade-offs that emerge from certain choices or what goods and services are sometimes scarce.

6–8

Ask students to select phrases to make the chants more complex with three layered lines. In order for this to work, they will need to experiment with rhythm, dynamics, pitch, and word choice. The first line becomes the base line of the chant, and the other lines layer on top. Students can create chants about the kinds of resistance people and groups have had to overcome in addition to social movements, such as labor movements.

Sample Chants

Tezcatlipoca

Out of the evening sky he came

Unseen, untouched

Ruler of the gods

Heart of the world

Views the world through the magic of his mirror

The Rescue

Musicians of the sun, hear my call!

I am coming to set you free

Stay where you are!

Continue to play!

Sun's rays burn

Howling wind blows

The chants were inspired by McDermott, Gerald. 1997. *Musicians of the Sun*. New York: Simon & Schuster Books for Young Readers.

Name _____ Date _____

Chant Planner

Directions: Discuss the questions with your group to plan for creating and performing your chant.

1. What does the folktale tell you about the culture of a group (beliefs, daily life, food, clothing, religion, etc.)?

   _____

   _____

   _____

2. What ideas will you include in your chant? Why?

   _____

   _____

   _____

3. What lines will you repeat? Why?

   _____

   _____

   _____

4. Find examples of figurative language, such as metaphor, simile, and alliteration, in the folktale. Will you include these phrases? Why or why not?

   _____

   _____

5. What information will you put in your own words, or paraphrase? Why?

   _____

   _____

Soundscapes

Model Lesson: Hearing the Historical Moment

Model Lesson Overview

In this lesson, students re-create a historical event or place with only sound. They create soundscapes in small groups or as a class to represent the mood, atmosphere, and significance of the historical moment in time, such as an ancient city, rural towns and urban cities, the Industrial Revolution, a weather event, or life "on the trail" as people migrated to different parts of the United States. They view primary source photographs, photo essays, film clips, paintings, or other sources that can be found on the Library of Congress website. Then, students bring the moment to life by creating sounds with their voices, found objects, or instruments and then layer the sounds to create a soundscape.

Standards

K–2

- Understands the causes and nature of movements of large groups of people into and within the United States, now and long ago

- Echoes short rhythms and melodic patterns

- Knows characteristics that make certain music suitable for specific uses

3–5

- Knows the reasons why Dust Bowl farm families migrated to different parts of the United States

- Creates and arranges music to accompany readings or dramatizations

- Improvises short songs and instrumental pieces using a variety of sound sources, including traditional sounds, nontraditional sounds, body sounds, and sounds produced by electronic means

6–8

- Understands the causes of the Great Depression and how it affected American society

- Knows how the elements of music are used to achieve unity and variety, tension and release, and balance in musical compositions

- Performs on an instrument accurately and independently, alone and in small and large ensembles

Soundscapes *(cont.)*

Materials

- Primary sources, such as photographs, sketches, and film clips of the historical moment of study

- Audio-recording software (*optional*)

- *Soundscape Planner* (page 124, soundscapeplanner.pdf)

Preparation

Locate primary source photographs or sketches about your chosen historical time period of study by visiting the Library of Congress website. Gather multiple photographs of the same historical moment in time and have groups choose a photograph to explore through sound. Determine if students will use found sounds or percussion instruments, such as triangles and drums, to create music. They can also create sounds using their voices. If students will be using instruments, gather them ahead of time. You can also have students use audio software to record their soundscapes. Students will need time to experiment with their instruments to discover the varied types of sounds they can produce. For instance, a cheese grater if scraped slowly with a pen could either sound like an engine revving up or a chirping cricket, but if tapped on the edge, it could sound like the halyard of a sailboat. Additional ideas are provided in the Specific Grade Level Ideas.

Procedure

1. Activate students' prior knowledge about patterns of migration throughout U.S. history. For example, if studying the experiences of those who moved from the Dust Bowl to California and other states, ask, "Why did some groups migrate to California? How did life change for these groups when they migrated?"

2. Share primary sources, such as photographs, to provide students with a wide lens on this time period. Consider studying the photographs of Dorothea Lange, who documented the hardships of migrating families during the Great Depression, which are available through the Library of Congress website. If possible, play audio or video clips by Woody Guthrie, whose music was shaped by the hardships of the time, many of which are available through the PBS website.

3. Tell students that they will explore the Great Depression using only sound by creating a soundscape. Divide students into groups based on the content. For example, you could divide students into groups representing the sounds of the Dust Bowl and the sounds of life after migration (e.g., the sounds of picking fruit or the sounds of shantytowns).

Soundscapes (cont.)

4. Distribute the *Soundscape Planner* (page 124) activity sheet to students. Provide each group with at least one primary source photograph so that they can mine the image for details that can be represented and expressed through sound. Use the Planning Questions to help students generate ideas.

5. Have groups use found sounds, percussion instruments, and/or vocals as they practice playing sounds together that represent the historical moment. Demonstrate with each group the difference between organizing the playing of their sounds and playing all the sounds at the same time.

6. Have all groups come together to form one ensemble and perform the soundscapes. If desired, record students' soundscapes, using any audio-recording software available to you.

7. Using the Questions for Discussion, explore with students how music helped them understand the content.

Planning Questions

- What is the meaning of *rhythm*, *tempo*, and *texture*? How could you consider these terms as you create your soundscapes?

- What is the mood or atmosphere of the environment you are re-creating?

- How will you re-create sounds in the most authentic way?

- How will you bring your audience into the environment you are re-creating as quickly as possible?

- Would you hear sounds in your chosen environment separately or together? Are the sounds continuous, or do they stop every so often?

- Will you ask the audience to close their eyes? Why or why not?

Questions for Discussion

- In what ways did the soundscapes help you understand the historical time and place?

- In what ways did the soundscape help you understand the mood and atmosphere of the environment you re-created?

- What activities, objects, and events helped you create the soundscape?

- How did the creation of a soundscape bring each distinct environment to life?

- What choices did you make in re-creating an environment through sound?

Soundscapes *(cont.)*

Specific Grade Level Ideas

K–2

Students can explore through sound what life was like for children "on the trail" when their families moved from one part of the United States to another and the causes of this movement. Have students explore aspects of children of migrant working families, using a book such as *Amelia's Road* by Linda Jacobs Altman. Students can also re-create the sounds of an ancient city, a rural town, an urban city, the Industrial Revolution, or a weather event.

3–5

Students can create soundscapes to understand how settlement patterns are influenced by the discovery and use of resources. For example, students could explore the sounds of Colorado mining towns as centers of settlement in the late 19th century. They could also investigate the growth of industry and cities along the fall line of the Appalachians starting in the 18th century. Soundscapes also help students understand differences in urban and rural children's lives in the early- and mid-19th century as they relate to industrialization.

6–8

Students can explore the symbolic importance of capital cities, such as Canberra, a planned city that is the capital of Australia, or The Hague as both a national capital of the Netherlands and a center for such global agencies as the International Court of Justice. They can also represent through sound the patterns of land use in urban, suburban, and rural areas.

Name _____ Date _____

Soundscape Planner

Directions: Complete the chart to plan for your soundscape. Look carefully at the photograph, sketch, historical painting, video clip, or other resource available to you. Think about the activities, objects, events, and sounds that might have been heard at the time.

How will you re-create these sounds?			
What sounds might have been heard?			
Describe the primary source. Consider the activities, events, and/or objects represented.			

Mash-Up

Model Lesson: Songs of the Past

Model Lesson Overview

In this lesson, students explore the meaning of songs from historical time periods. They choose two songs from the time period of study and record a portion of the lyrics. Then, they combine the lyrics from the two songs to create a mash-up, extending their understanding of the themes communicated through song. By creating mash-ups, students learn how songs capture the struggles, hopes, and resiliency of people of the past.

Standards

K–2

- Understands the relationship between music and history and culture

- Knows characteristics that make certain music suitable for specific uses

- Knows that music comes from different places and different periods of time

3–5

- Knows that families long ago expressed and transmitted their beliefs and values through songs, hymns, and proverbs

- Understands how songs describe the struggles of people in various regions of the country

- Identifies music from various historical periods and cultures

- Knows that all cultures use the same basic elements of music in their music

6–8

- Understands characteristics of works in various art forms that share similar subject matter, historical periods, or cultural context

- Understands distinguishing characteristics of representative music genres from a variety of cultures

9–12

- Knows how characteristics of the arts vary within a particular historical period or style and how these characteristics relate to ideas, issues, or themes in other disciplines

- Classifies unfamiliar but representative aural examples of music

Mash-Up *(cont.)*

Materials

- Song lyrics from the period of study

- Examples of mash-ups

- *Meaning of the Lyrics* (page 129, meaninglyrics.pdf)

- *Mash-Up Planner* (page 130, mashupplanner.pdf)

Preparation

In the days and weeks prior to this lesson, familiarize students with the lyrics and melodies of multiple songs from the time period of study. The Library of Congress website offers themed resources and primary source sets, including sheet music that your students can view. If studying the slavery of African Americans in the South and the songs that tell of the experiences of slaves, visit http://www.pbs.org/wgbh/amex/singers/sfeature/songs.html. Print copies of song lyrics that students have researched or are familiar with.

Locate examples of mash-ups online and bookmark them so that you can readily share them with students to give a sense of how mash-ups work. Additional ideas are provided in the Specific Grade Level Ideas.

Procedure

1. Activate students' prior knowledge, using questions about the historical and cultural influence of songs, such as, "How can songs uplift and inspire a group? How do songs teach us about experiences of the past?"

2. Tell students that they will search for common themes among songs from the same time period. Define musical terms that you will be referencing, such as *melody* (the tune of a song), *lyrics* (the words in a song), and *chorus* (the repeating lines of a song).

3. Divide students into groups of two or more. Distribute copies of a variety of song lyrics from the time period of study. Distribute the *Meaning of the Lyrics* (page 129) activity sheet to each group. Direct students to choose two songs and complete the *Meaning of the Lyrics* activity sheet.

4. Share with students some examples of mash-ups. Distribute the *Mash-Up Planner* (page 130) activity sheet to students and have them work in their groups to focus on the themes and messages communicated in their two chosen songs and create a new composition by combining the lyrics in a new way. Use the Planning Questions to stimulate students' thinking.

5. Have students sing or play the musical mash-up in order to hear how the two melodies alternate and work together.

Mash-Up *(cont.)*

6. Encourage students to share their mash-ups with the class.

7. Discuss the process with students using the Questions for Discussion.

Planning Questions

- What lyrics will you select? Why?

- How will you piece the lyrics together in a new way?

- How might you highlight the messages of the two songs?

- What different combinations and arrangements will you try?

Questions for Discussion

- What did the songs teach you about the people and events of the time period?

- What common themes did you find throughout two or more songs from the same time period?

- What decisions did you make in creating a mash-up?

- How is your mash-up meaningful?

Specific Grade Level Ideas

K–2

Using the chorus lyrics from two songs, work as a class to create a mash-up. Have students write about the meaning. Consider using familiar songs that teach about the past, such as patriotic songs.

3–5

Have students write about the messages communicated in their mash-ups. Students can explore songs of the Industrial Revolution, including coal mining, and create mash-ups to show the different struggles and experiences of the time period that share common themes.

Mash-Up *(cont.)*

6–8

Students can create mash-ups to understand the struggle for racial and gender equality and for the extension of civil liberties. They can explore through song the period of slavery when there were free and enslaved people of African descent who sang many of the same songs, mostly because enslaved and free people practiced the same religion. They can explore labor movements and include the unofficial anthem of the civil rights movement, "We Shall Overcome." Students could also use mash-ups to explore child labor from the past to the present-day global economy. Consider using *Sugar Changed the World* by Marc Aronson and Marina Budhos and visit http://sugarchangedtheworld.com/ to understand the trans-Atlantic African slave trade, hear the songs of the time of the sugar plantations in South America and the Caribbean Islands, and explore the messages they communicate.

9–12

In addition to the 6–8 Specific Grade Levels Ideas, students can explore the ways that people resisted Nazi policies and orders by creating mash-ups of time-period songs about the Holocaust.

Name _____ Date _____

Meaning of the Lyrics

Directions: Complete the chart to explore common themes of songs from your time period of study. Themes may include *hope*, *fear*, *protest*, *longing for the past*, *faith*, *freedom*, or *unification*.

Time period of study:	Song #1 title and composer:	Song #2 title and composer:
Lyrics to the chorus or another group of lyrics in the song		
What are the themes communicated?		

Name _____ Date _____

Mash-Up Planner

Directions: Use the chart to help you create a new composition with a portion of the lyrics from two or more songs of the same time period.

Song # 1 selected lyrics:

Song #2 selected lyrics:

Piece the lyrics together in a new way. Consider how you can emphasize the messages of the songs. Try a few different combinations to explore the choices and different arrangements of melodies.

Poetry

#51092—*Strategies to Integrate the Arts in Social Studies* © *Shell Education*

Poetry

Understanding Poetry

Poetry engages students in writing, reading, speaking, and listening. Creating poems can capture the essence of an idea. As stated by Polly Collins, "When students create poems about topics of study, they enhance their comprehension through the connections they have made between the topic and their own lives, the topic and the world around them, and the poetry and the content texts they have read" (2008, 83).

Exploring history through the writing of poetry allows students to consider historic or geographic concepts in new ways and share their understanding through language and metaphor. Often, students enjoy creating poems but are not sure how to begin. The strategies provide guidance that will help students identify and work with rich language to explore ideas and deepen comprehension.

Though many historic poems or lyrics often rhyme, they do not need to, and sentences don't need to always be complete. "We are more interested in 'surprising images' or words that have a special sound pattern. They empower students to be 'word-gatherers'" (McKim and Steinbergh 1992, 45). Students are invited to put words together in unconventional ways, drawing on evocative language, playful juxtaposition of ideas, and creating images through words as they write poems about concepts in geography, history, and world history. This active engagement changes students' relationships with social studies as they find their own language to describe what they know.

Strategies for Poetry

∞ Dialogue Poems

Compare and contrast is one of the most effective instructional strategies that teachers can use (Marzano 2007). A dialogue poem encourages students to explore two different perspectives on a topic in history, world history, or geography. This form of poetry works well with opposite but related concepts or perspectives as in the multiple views and voices of different populations affected by world wars or environmental changes. Similarities and differences between historical periods or moments can be explored, providing the rhythm and the feel of a dialogue. The poem is constructed by two writers, encouraging conversation about the social studies content being explored and the ways to best translate ideas into poetic form. This collaborative work allows students to share what they know about history or geography with their peers while engaging in writing activities that deepen social studies learning. Students can brainstorm ideas in groups to create their own dialogue poems that bring a geographical or environmental issue to life. These poems also prompt students to better differentiate between two concepts that are being learned at the same time.

∞ Rhyme and Rhythm

This strategy invites students to explore and experiment with the sounds of words as they investigate rhythms, asking questions such as, "What patterns feel regular? What patterns change?" Students decide what they like about rhyming and nonrhyming poems. Jan LaBonty notes that "a preference for rhyme and rhythm is contained in the linguistic make-up of all humans; rhyme is easier to recall than prose; rhythm helps carry the predictability of language. There is pattern and measure in every language and in the way we structure our lives" (1997).

Though poems do not need to rhyme, rhymes can unify a poem, and the repeated sound can help to connect a concept in one line to that in another. Also, simple rhymes can serve as a memory device (Jensen 2008). Students are even more likely to remember poems they create themselves, and using rhyme and/or rhythm to create their poems allows students to synthesize learning and distill the essence of concepts and ideas.

Poetry *(cont.)*

ೞ Juxtaposition

This strategy prompts students to find and collect words and phrases from a variety of sources. Students collect and record these words on paper and place them in a "word bowl." Students draw out the words and phrases, playing with the juxtaposition of the words. They experiment with line breaks and the creation of meaning in unexpected ways, revealing fresh language and insights into the concepts of study. McKim and Steinbergh note that with word-bowl poetry, "the very fact of manipulating the words, discarding some, trading others, adding what one needs for sense, can teach us something about selection and choice in making poems. Joining two or three words that normally don't appear together can make fresh images, charging them with new energy and excitement" (1992, 38).

This strategy allows students to work with descriptions of concepts to create poems that reveal relationships and ideas about content in unique and enlightening language. Putting words together through juxtaposition allows students to boil ideas down to their essence. Students will benefit from having a range of words available from which to draw.

ೞ Structured Poems

There are many forms of poetry that are created within specified formats. The structure of a certain number of words and syllables or a given pattern of rhythm helps students plan and organize their writing about social studies concepts. JoAnne Growney notes that "long traditions embrace the fourteen-line sonnet with its ten-syllable lines. Five-line limericks and seventeen-syllable haiku also are familiar forms. Moreover, patterns of accent and rhyme overlay the line and syllable counts for even more intricacy" (2009, 12). The possibilities are endless as students engage with different patterns and writing within a particular structure, enabling social studies concepts to be viewed through a new lens. Furthermore, Corie Herman (2003) suggests that the structured nature of these poems supports diverse students' abilities to succeed in writing them.

ೞ Bio Poems

Bio poems often follow a pattern and can be created through student responses to prompts (Kuta 2003). Using the senses to reflect on what has been seen, heard, smelled, touched, and tasted, students become aware of how they (or characters, fictional or real) have been shaped by their unique experiences. This biographical strategy allows students to investigate traditions, attitudes, environmental influences, and commonly held perceptions about a particular idea or within a particular era. The observations and reflections help students become aware of how time and place can influence perspective. When written about themselves, students' bio poems can provide teachers with relevant background information, offer insights into how to best work with individual students, and enhance student–teacher communication.

Dialogue Poems

Model Lesson: People and the Environment

Model Lesson Overview

In this strategy, students read mentor poems written for two voices and then work in pairs to create dialogue poems that show differing perspectives about a concept. Concepts explored may include how human actions modify the physical environment, how physical systems affect human systems, or other historical ideas, such as the process of compromise or the problem-solving abilities and traits demonstrated by many historical figures. In creating dialogue poems, students gain a deeper understanding of the similarities and differences between two sides of an issue.

Standards

K–2

- Knows how people affect the environment in negative and positive ways

- Knows ways people depend on the environment

- Knows the main ideas or theme of a story, drama, or poem

3–5

- Knows the ways in which the physical environment is stressed by human activities

- Knows how differences in perception affect people's interpretations of the world

- Knows the defining characteristics and structural elements of a variety of literary genres

6–8

- Understands the environmental consequences of people changing the physical environment

- Knows the defining features and structural elements of a variety of literary genres

9–12

- Knows changes in the physical environment that have reduced the capacity of the environment to support human activity

- Understands how people who live in naturally hazardous regions adapt to their environments

- Knows the defining characteristics of a variety of literary forms and genres

Dialogue Poems (cont.)

Materials

- *Example Dialogue Poem* (page 141, dialoguepoem.pdf)
- Primary and secondary sources about the topic of study
- *Two Voices Poem Plan* (page 142, twovoicesplan.pdf)
- Audio-recording software (*optional*)

Preparation

Prior to the lesson, discuss the perspectives of a topic of study and how the perspectives are similar and different. If studying geographical topics, consider two points of view about pollution of the ocean (e.g., big oil company representative versus the natural life forms and habitats in the ocean). Brainstorm characteristics of each perspective in preparation for a class discussion. Familiarize yourself with the *Example Dialogue Poem* (page 141) activity sheet or try writing one of your own. Each "side" of the poem is read by a different voice, and the lines in italics are read by both voices. Gather primary and secondary sources about the topic that express two opposing points of view. Additional ideas are provided in the Specific Grade Level Ideas.

Procedure

1. Display the *Example Dialogue Poem* (page 141) activity sheet for students, or share your own. Explain that the lines in italics are read by both voices. Have two students read the poem for the class, both voicing a role in the poem.

2. Ask students, "What do you notice about how this poem is written? How does the poem reveal contrasting ideas? Shared ideas? What do you notice about the quality of the spoken lines when they are read by both voices?"

3. As a class, brainstorm a list of possible contrasting ideas about your topic of study, and record the list for students to reference throughout the lesson. Encourage students to use the primary and secondary sources to draw out more ideas and language that could be woven into the poems.

4. Divide students into pairs. Allow each pair to choose an idea for their dialogue poem from the brainstormed list.

5. Distribute the *Two Voices Poem Plan* (page 142) activity sheet to each pair, and provide enough time for them to write their own dialogue poems. Circulate among the pairs and use the Planning Questions to guide discussion. Encourage students to create an image to further exemplify the concepts.

6. As students develop their poems, encourage them to consider the content and order of the concepts they have included. Have them revise their poems based on both content and how it sounds when read aloud by two voices. Allow time for students to practice performing their poems aloud.

Dialogue Poems *(cont.)*

7. Invite students to record their performances, using audio-recording software, and listen and discuss the recording. You can also share these poems on a class blog.

8. Have each pair present their poem to the class. Use the Questions for Discussion to guide discussion.

Planning Questions

- What words or phrases are associated with either idea?

- How do the perspectives differ? What ideas do the perspectives share?

- What lines and concepts could the voices share?

- What powerful word choices will you use?

- How will you embed examples from social studies within the poem?

- How will your poem illustrate the differences between these perspectives?

Questions for Discussion

- What differences did you identify between the viewpoints?

- What did you learn by writing your poem?

- In what ways does poetry help us understand a concept?

- What feedback could you give about the other students' poems?

Specific Grade Level Ideas

K–2

Students can write dialogue poems to explore the similarities and differences between various folk heroes or to understand the school experiences of the past and today. They can write dialogue poems to compare and contrast cities and farms or to classify regions based on landforms and climate. Students can write a dialogue poem in which either voice is located on a different side of the globe (North Pole and South Pole) or speak from two coasts on a map. They can show how important figures reacted to their times and why they were significant to the history of our country, or they can show the different ways people communicate with one another now and in the past and the technological developments that facilitate communication. Students studying economics can write from different perspectives on the scarcity of resources and opportunity costs and how people must make choices about using goods and services to satisfy needs and wants.

Dialogue Poems *(cont.)*

3–5

Students can write dialogue poems to explore the origins of various groups that immigrated to the United States and why various immigrant groups left their countries of origin. They can compare and contrast songs, symbols, and slogans that demonstrate freedom of expression and the role of democracy. Dialogue poetry is a powerful way to understand the roles of significant historical figures and the idea of compromise. Students can also write poems about the perspectives of Americans who strived for independence from England versus the king of England.

Students can also use their knowledge about how to find absolute locations using latitude and longitude on maps to create dialogue poems about the differences and similarities of specific locations. Students can write dialogue poems to compare and contrast how regions are similar and different in form and function (e.g., local neighborhoods versus central business districts).

6–8

Students can write dialogue poems to explore the perspectives and roles played by various groups of people such as free and enslaved people of African descent, Native Americans, and white settlers, or the varied experiences of women and men during the American Revolution. Students can create dialogue poems describing the impact of transportation systems on residents of urban neighborhoods living close to trains, airports, or factories.

Dialogue poetry allows students to examine perspectives involved in historical and present-day domestic and foreign politics. Students studying economics can develop their understanding of how scarcity of resources requires choice at both the personal and the societal level by showing differing and shared perspectives in their poetry. Students can also consider treaties and other efforts to achieve peace and recovery during World War I, such as the conflicting aims and aspirations of the countries involved in the Treaty of Versailles and how the major powers responded to the terms of the settlement, why and how the League of Nations was founded and its initial goals and limitations, the nations that were and were not invited to participate in the League of Nations, and the changes made to political boundaries after the peace treaties that ended World War I.

Dialogue Poems *(cont.)*

9–12

In addition to the 6–8 Specific Grade Level Ideas, students can write dialogue poems considering the moral dilemmas involved in the Holocaust, such as a Nazi officer who goes home to play with his children or the question of stealing bread and medicine to survive. Students can also write dialogue poems to examine the conflicting thoughts and struggles within one person about a wide variety of social and political themes.

Example Dialogue Poem

"Intelligent Species: A Poem for Two Voices"

by David Williams

Dolphin   **Human**

I hear they're a very intelligent species

They love their families

They love to play

In times of trouble, they work together

To protect one another

To solve problems

Their communication is quite advanced

With a sophisticated lexicon

With nuance of meaning

We have so much in common

But they do not care for us

But they do not understand

What matters most

Is this beautiful world

Is the bottom line

I hear they're very intelligent, so they must understand

That the gulf is a treasure

That the gulf is a gold mine

That biomes are fragile

That accidents happen

That what matters most is survival

We are ensnared in your nets

We face a net loss

Oil covers our skin

The price of oil is dropping

They will change their ways

They will understand

If

Humans

Dolphins

Are a very intelligent species

Name _____ Date _____

Two Voices Poem Plan

Directions: Use this planning sheet to brainstorm ideas for your poem. Be sure to consider how the perspectives are different in addition to the ideas they might share. Then, draft your poem on a separate sheet of paper.

Concept: _____

Poem Title: _____

Voice 1
Words and Phrases:

_____

_____

_____

_____

Voice 2
Words and Phrases:

_____

_____

_____

_____

Combined Voices
Words and Phrases:

_____

_____

_____

_____

Rhyme and Rhythm

Model Lesson: World History Monument Poems

Model Lesson Overview

In this lesson, students explore rhyme and rhythm by reading rhyming and nonrhyming historical poems. They write their own poems about historical information. Students research and collect information about historical monuments and then embed it in poems incorporating rhyme and/or rhythm to bring the monuments to life in new ways.

Standards

K–2

- Understands that sculptures can reflect the daily life, history, and beliefs of a country
- Knows rhyming sounds and simple rhymes

3–5

- Knows important buildings, statues, and monuments in the state's history
- Knows the defining characteristics and structural elements of a variety of literary genres
- Understands the ways in which language is used in literary texts

6–8

- Understands that specific individuals and the values those individuals held had an impact on history
- Understands the use of language in literary works to convey mood, images, and meaning

Materials

- Rhyming and nonrhyming poems about famous historical places, events, monuments, etc.
- *My Poem About History* (page 147, poemabouthistory.pdf)

Rhyme and Rhythm *(cont.)*

Preparation

Identify poems about famous places or monuments relating to world history. Locate at least two poems (rhyming and nonrhyming) that focus on historical information. The Poetry Foundation (http://www.poetryfoundation.org) provides poems by theme. Consider "Facing It" by Yusef Komunyakaa, which is about a visit to the Vietnam War Memorial, or "Concord Hymn" by Ralph Waldo Emerson, which was sung at the completion of the Battle Monument in 1837. Also consider "The Negro Speaks of Rivers" by Langston Hughes or "Paris in Spring" by Sara Teasdale. These poems contain historical information about monuments or places and embed history in imagery, sensory details, metaphor, and rhyme and rhythm. Additional ideas are provided in the Specific Grade Level Ideas.

Procedure

1. Read one of your chosen poems aloud to students. As you read the poem, ask students to pay particular attention to the poem's sensory connections, historical ideas, themes, the rhythm of the poem, and whether it follows a rhyme scheme. Discuss these elements of the poem with students. Focus on what is communicated through rhyme and/or rhythm when the poem is read aloud.

2. Display the poem for students to see and ask them to identify what makes the poem memorable. Discuss any rhyming words, rhythm, images, sensory details, and the way ideas are communicated.

3. Then, repeat this process with a second poem so students recognize that poets use a variety of styles when writing poetry.

4. Tell students that they are going to write their own poems about famous places or monuments and how they relate to history. Have students choose partners, and assign each pair a place or monument or allow students to choose their own.

5. Have students work together to brainstorm ideas for their poems and decide on a style of rhythm and/or rhyme. Invite them to share their ideas with the class.

6. Tell students that they will use the ideas they brainstormed with their partners to write their own individual poem. Distribute the *My Poem About History* (page 147) activity sheet and invite students to use it to write their poems. Use the Planning Questions to facilitate discussion and planning.

7. Once students have created their poems, encourage them to practice reading the poems aloud to experiment with the rhythm and/or rhyme.

8. Have students read their poems to their partners or to the whole class. Use the Questions for Discussion to debrief.

Rhyme and Rhythm *(cont.)*

Planning Questions

- What historical concept will you bring to life in your poem?

- What do you want your reader to imagine and remember?

- What ideas do you have for powerful word choices?

- Will you write a poem that rhymes or a poem that does not rhyme?

- How might you create rhythm and beat?

Questions for Discussion

- How is a poem different from other forms of writing?

- Why might a poet choose to use rhyme?

- How did you use rhyme and/or rhythm to bring historical ideas to life in your own poem?

- How do poems add context to historical information?

Specific Grade Level Ideas

K–2

Students can explore rhyme and rhythm by writing poems about famous landmarks, monuments, or constructions, such as the Eiffel Tower in Paris, the mysterious statues of Easter Island, The Statue of Liberty, or Mount Rushmore.

Students could explore historical concepts using rhythm and rhyme to write poems about scientific and technological achievements throughout history, such as the invention of paper in China, Mayan calendars, mummification in Egypt, astronomical discoveries in the Muslim world, or the invention of the steam engine in England.

Rhyme and Rhythm *(cont.)*

3–5

Gather images of famous large-scale creations from world history (e.g., the pyramids of Egypt, the Palais de Versaille in France, the Taj Mahal in India, or the Golden Gate Bridge in San Francisco, California). Allow students to first make their own observations about places and monuments and then research areas they wish to know more about. Poems can then be written based on their visual and research-based investigations.

Students can write rhyming and nonrhyming poems with rhythm to explore ideas about geography, such as the location of natural and human features and places, and changing transportation and communication technologies.

6–8

Students can use rhyme and rhythm to explore the accomplishments of famous Roman citizens who have been immortalized in giant statues and buildings, or they can explore the causes of various events in history such as the American Revolution and the idea of "taxation without representation." They can also write poems with rhyme and/or rhythm to consider the main ideas of historical and current-day documents and policies.

Name _____   Date _____

My Poem About History

Directions: Use the chart to brainstorm ideas for a history poem.

My topic:

Ideas from my research (images, facts, interesting details):

Ideas I would like to incorporate in my poem:

Ideas for rhyme and/or rhythm:

Juxtaposition

Model Lesson: Innovations in History

Model Lesson Overview

In this lesson, students research, collect, and brainstorm words they associate with history concepts and put the words together in new ways to create poems that depict historical understanding. Students are encouraged to experiment with a variety of ways to juxtapose the words and add more words and phrases to extend learning.

Standards

K–2

- Knows that people are always inventing new ways to solve problems and accomplish work

- Uses prewriting strategies to plan written work

- Uses descriptive words to convey basic ideas

- Uses writing and other methods to describe familiar persons, places, objects, or experiences

3–5

- Knows that people have invented and used tools throughout history to solve problems and improve ways of doing things

- Uses prewriting strategies to plan written work

- Uses descriptive and precise language that clarifies and enhances ideas

6–8

- Knows that invention is the process of creating a new system or object out of an idea while innovation is the process of modifying an existing system or object to improve it

- Uses a variety of prewriting strategies

- Uses descriptive language that clarifies and enhances ideas

Materials

- Small boxes, bowls, or other containers

- *Poetry Word List* (page 152, wordlist.pdf)

- Microphone (*optional*)

Juxtaposition *(cont.)*

Preparation

Select a few world history innovations that students are familiar with but could deepen their understanding about, such as the printing press or the wheel. Have students investigate these innovations in the days and weeks prior to this lesson. Collect small boxes, bowls, or other containers to use as "word bowls" from which students will draw out words for poems. Additional ideas are provided in the Specific Grade Level Ideas.

Procedure

1. After students have investigated and read about particular innovations, brainstorm words and short phrases as a class that are associated with a single innovation. Record brainstormed words and phrases so that students can refer to them throughout the lesson.

2. Ask students to help you create a class poem by selecting words and phrases from the brainstormed list and arranging them in a poem in new and interesting ways. Explain that the idea is to put the words together and experiment with the line breaks in a variety of ways until a clear sense of the idea being explored is expressed. Encourage the use of metaphors, similes, imagery, sensory descriptions, and feeling words.

3. Divide students into small groups and assign or allow groups to choose an innovation. Distribute the *Poetry Word List* (page 152) activity sheet and have groups collect words and short phrases to build their own lists from newspaper articles, magazines, historical fiction, or any other related texts. If desired, have students conduct research about their innovation and mine the resources for powerful words and phrases for their lists.

4. Provide each group with a box, a bowl, or another container to serve as a word bowl. Have students cut their words apart and place them in the word bowl.

5. Ask students to draw out a few words from the bowl to begin and work together to juxtapose the words in different ways to write a group poem. Remind students to pay careful attention to how the juxtaposition of the words impacts meaning. Tell groups that the selected words and phrases are just a starting point to spark ideas. They can choose not to use certain words, they can draw additional words from the bowl, or they can add words and phrases they prefer.

6. Once poems are completed, have each group write a final version to share with the class. Students can also add images to illustrate the ideas.

7. Allow time for students to rehearse reading their poems aloud to bring them to life.

Juxtaposition *(cont.)*

8. Plan a poetry slam when students can present their poems to one another. If desired, bring in a microphone and invite other classes to hear the poems.

9. Use the Questions for Discussion to debrief.

Questions for Discussion

- What choices did you make in selecting words and phrases to use in your poem?

- What did you learn through the process of creating your own poem?

- What unique or fresh language resulted from juxtaposing different words and phrases?

- What made a compelling poem?

- What did you learn about your world history innovation?

- What did you learn from listening to the poems of others?

Specific Grade Level Ideas

K–2

Students can collect words for their word bowl by mining magazines and newspaper articles with large print. They can choose words and phrases that will summarize the content of the article. Students can also collect words from primary and secondary sources related to the history of their local community. For example, they can brainstorm words by viewing a primary source photograph of an old school building in the community. They could also brainstorm words as a class to describe geographical ideas about local rivers, lakes, historic sites, and landforms.

3–5

In addition to the K–2 Specific Grade Level Ideas, students can collect and record words from regional folktales, stories, and songs that have contributed to the development of the cultural history of the United States. They could also collect words for their word bowls from powerful excerpts in historical fiction texts or historical documents. Students can collect words from current-event newscasts, radio shows, podcasts, and blog entries about issues such as environmental efforts or elections.

Juxtaposition *(cont.)*

6–8

Students can collect words from newspaper articles of the past to explore the Allies' response to the Holocaust and to understand President Roosevelt's immigration policy toward Jewish refugees from Nazi Germany. Have students mine the newspaper articles to collect words that they can arrange into powerful poems.

Students can also mine articles and collect words about the history of the Internet, its impact on their daily lives, and what it has made possible in terms of communication and creativity.

Name _____ Date _____

Poetry Word List

Directions: Record words and phrases about your topic in the spaces. Then, cut out the words and place them in a word bowl. Draw out a few words and arrange them in different ways. Play with the arrangement to create meaning, mood, and rhythm.

My collection of words and phrases:

Structured Poems

Model Lesson: Cinquains from Greek History

Model Lesson Overview

The cinquain structure prompts students to make careful choices about how best to represent ideas and distill their thinking. This poem structure guides writers in using a sequence of words, types of words, and syllables on each line. Students write cinquain poems to reflect on historical world concepts, such as Greek gods and goddesses, or to examine present-day issues, such as the protection and conservation of nature. Student writers explore how rhythm and word choice communicate meaning and the mood associated with ideas in social studies.

Standards

K–2

- Understands the daily life, history, and beliefs of a country as reflected in dance, music, or the other art forms

- Knows the main ideas or theme of a story, drama, or poem

3–5

- Understands that specific ideas had an impact on history

- Understands the major cultural elements of Greek society

- Understands the ways in which language is used in literary texts

6–8

- Analyzes the influence that specific ideas and beliefs had on history

- Understands the role of art, literature, and mythology in Greek society

- Understands the use of language in literary works to convey mood, images, and meaning

Materials

- Collection of primary and secondary sources about the topic of study
- *Word-Count Cinquain Planner* (page 158, cinquainplanner1.pdf)
- *Parts of Speech Cinquain Planner* (page 159, cinquainplanner2.pdf)
- *Syllables Cinquain Planner* (page 160, cinquainplanner3.pdf)
- *Cinquain Examples* (page 157, cinquainexamples.pdf)

Structured Poems *(cont.)*

Preparation

Compile a collection of primary and secondary source materials to support students' research on the concept of study, such as Greek gods and goddesses and the ideals and origins of Greek tragedies and philosophies. Supportive materials may include texts about art history, images of Greek sculpture, and myths. Try writing cinquain poems yourself to experience the structures shown in the *Word-Count Cinquain Planner* (page 158), the *Parts of Speech Cinquain Planner* (page 159), and the *Syllables Cinquain Planner* (page 160) activity sheets that students will be using. Additional ideas are provided in the Specific Grade Level Ideas.

Procedure

1. Display the *Cinquain Examples* (page 157) activity sheet for students or share cinquains of your own creation. Read the poems to students, have students read along with you, or ask student volunteers to read them aloud. Then, read the poems to students again, asking listeners to consider the rhythm, word choices, and mood and to identify how the poem brings a historical idea to life.

2. Choose a topic related to social studies, such as Greek mythology or architecture, and invite students to brainstorm words associated with this topic, recording a list of words for students to reference throughout the lesson. Ask students to collect words and phrases as they conduct research on the topic, drawing from primary and secondary sources.

3. Display the *Word-Count Cinquain Planner* (page 158), the *Parts of Speech Cinquain Planner* (page 159), or the *Syllables Cinquain Planner* (page 160) activity sheet, whichever is most appropriate for your students. As a class, work through ideas for the different lines of the poem, drawing from the list of brainstormed words.

4. Divide students into small groups, and have each group create a cinquain poem that builds on the ideas generated. Circulate among the groups and use the Planning Questions to help students create images and use their senses. Note that these poem structures are not meant to be formulaic but rather utilized as structures to spark creativity. The cinquain structure prompts students to make careful choices about how best to represent ideas and distill their thinking.

5. Have each group read its cinquain poem aloud to the class. Use the Questions for Discussion to debrief the activity.

Structured Poems *(cont.)*

Planning Questions

- What is most important to express about your topic?

- Who is your audience?

- How will you create an image for the reader?

- What related words will you choose for the first and last lines?

- What ideas from your research give new insights about the ideas?

- How will you create mood and rhythm that enhances meaning?

Questions for Discussion

- What choices did you make as you selected words and phrases for your poem?

- What did you learn from the poems read by other groups?

- What language was most compelling?

- How did the sound and rhythm of your poem help communicate meaning?

- What are the main ideas communicated about each topic?

- How does writing a poem compare to sharing ideas in essays or book chapters?

Specific Grade Level Ideas

K–2

Students can write cinquain poems about geographical and environmental issues. For example, through cinquain, they can communicate the message that natural resources are "gifts of nature" because they are present without human intervention. Students could consider ideas about marine transportation by writing cinquains focused on the Erie Canal and its technology or the activities of people along the Erie Canal, or they can explore the development of the wheel and its early uses in ancient societies. Or students could write cinquains to represent the significance of a holiday or ceremony from different societies, including harvest and spring festivals.

Structured Poems *(cont.)*

3–5

In addition to the K–2 Specific Grade Level Ideas, students can write cinquain poetry about the characteristics of landforms, vegetation, or manufacturing. Writing cinquains helps students think deeply about their state's history. They can write poems about a state's symbol, slogan, motto, important buildings, statues, or monuments. They could write about life in a pioneer farming community such as the Old Northwest, the prairies, the Southwest, eastern Canada, or the Far West.

6–8

Students can explore ideas around social change, social movements, and civil rights, such as the Chicano Movement. They can consider the American Labor Movement and workforce conditions of the late 19th century, including how working conditions changed and how workers responded to new industrial conditions. Students can look at the connections between Greek culture, art, and architecture and how values and philosophy are reflected in the art and design of the time. For example, students could write cinquains inspired by the famous painting *The School of Athens* by Raphael near 1510, during what is considered the High Renaissance in Europe. This work contains many of the figures responsible for the most well-known ideas and innovations in Western thought and civilization.

Cinquain Examples

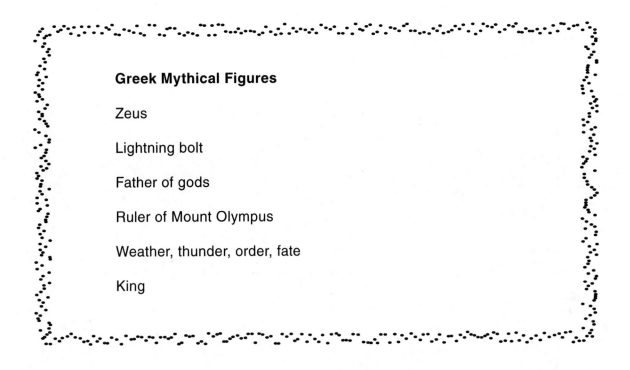

Greek Mythical Figures

Zeus

Lightning bolt

Father of gods

Ruler of Mount Olympus

Weather, thunder, order, fate

King

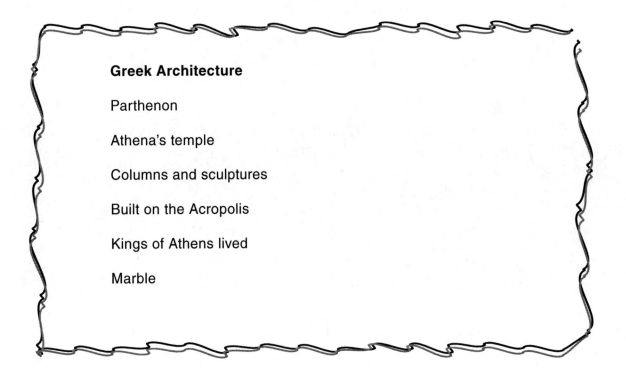

Greek Architecture

Parthenon

Athena's temple

Columns and sculptures

Built on the Acropolis

Kings of Athens lived

Marble

Name _____ Date _____

Word-Count Cinquain Planner

Directions: Collect words about your topic of study. Then, use the cinquain structure to create a poem. Experiment with different word choices.

Topic for my poem: _____

_____

Word collection: _____

_____

_____

My poem:

Title: _____

One word: _____

Two words: _____ _____

Three words: _____ _____ _____

Four words: _____ _____ _____ _____

One word: _____

Name _____ Date _____

Parts of Speech Cinquain Planner

Directions: Collect words about your topic of study. Then, use the cinquain structure to create a poem. Experiment with different word choices.

Topic for my poem: _____

_____

Word collection: _____

_____

_____

My poem:

Title: _____

Adjectives: _____ _____

-ing words: _____ _____ _____

Phrase: _____ _____ _____ _____

Synonym for title word: _____

#51092—Strategies to Integrate the Arts in Social Studies **159**

Name _____ Date _____

Syllables Cinquain Planner

Directions: Collect words about your topic of study. Then, use the cinquain structure to create a poem. Experiment with different word choices.

Topic for my poem: _____

_____

Word collection: _____

_____

_____

My poem:

Title: _____

Two syllables: ____ ____

Four syllables: ____ ____ ____ ____

Six syllables: ____ ____ ____ ____ ____ ____

Eight syllables: ____ ____ ____ ____ ____ ____ ____ ____

Two syllables: ____ ____

Bio Poems

Model Lesson: I Am From History

Model Lesson Overview

This particular approach to a bio poem is called an "I Am From" poem. In writing these poems, students take on the points of view of historical figures and consider the influences in their lives, the turning points, and the time periods in which they lived. "I Am From" poems were developed by teacher and writer George Ella Lyon (2010) and suggest a simple writing prompt for exploring personal histories and influences. Students begin each line with the phrase *I am from* and then introduce specific details of the individuals' lives such as special people, places, objects, influences, cultural traditions, foods, and sayings.

Standards

K–2

- Understands the contributions and significance of historical figures of the community

- Uses prewriting strategies to plan written work

- Uses descriptive words to convey basic ideas

3–5

- Understands how the ideas of significant people affected the history of the state

- Uses prewriting strategies to plan written work

- Uses descriptive and precise language that clarifies and enhances ideas

6–8

- Understands that specific individuals and the values those individuals held had an impact on history

- Uses a variety of prewriting strategies

- Uses descriptive language that clarifies and enhances ideas

9–12

- Analyzes the values held by specific people who influenced history and the role their values played in influencing history

- Conveys individual voice, tone, and point of view in writing

Materials

- *I Am From History Poem Example, K–5* (page 166, iamfromK–5.pdf) or *I Am From History Poem Example, 6–12* (page 167, iamfrom6–12.pdf)

- *I Am From History Planner* (page 168, iamfromplanner.pdf)

Bio Poems *(cont.)*

Preparation

Read the *I Am From History Poem Example, K–5* (page 166) or *I Am From History Poem Example, 6–12* (page 167) to become familiar with how the format can be used to write about a historical figure. You may wish to write your own "I Am From" poem to share with students. In the days and weeks prior to this lesson, assign or have students choose and conduct research about a historical figure, focusing on important life moments and experiences. Additional ideas are provided in the Specific Grade Level Ideas.

Procedure

1. Introduce the notion of being "from" someplace. Have students tell how they would respond to someone who asks casually, "Where are you from?" Then, have them discuss what would be different if a good friend asked, "So, how did you get to be you?"

2. Explain to students that they will think and write about a significant figure in world history. They will write a biography, or life story, from this person's perspective in the form of an "I Am From" poem.

3. Read aloud the *I Am From History Poem Example, K–5* (page 166), *I Am From History Poem Example, 6–12* (page 167), or your own "I Am From" poem, whichever is developmentally appropriate for your students. Discuss the ways in which the writers describe the subject's life experiences.

4. Assign or allow students to choose a significant figure in world history about whom to write a poem. Distribute the *I Am From History Planner* (page 168) activity sheet and have students discuss the various categories and possible responses. Consider adding additional prompts based on specific figures you are working with. Review the poem(s) you read in relation to the *I Am From History Planner*.

5. Allow time for students to reflect and record words, phrases, or sentences about their historical figures.

6. Have students use their brainstormed words and phrases to create their own "I Am From" poems about a historical figure. Make sure students understand that they do not have to include all of the topics or all of the words they brainstormed within a single poem. Circulate among students and use the Planning Questions to guide students' work.

7. Provide time for students to edit or confer about their poems in pairs and practice presenting their poems orally to one another. Then, have students share their poems with the class. Use the Questions for Discussion to lead discussion about the poems.

Bio Poems (cont.)

Planning Questions

- Who are the people who influenced your historical figure? How?

- What are the places or settings that influenced your historical figure?

- What important story does the historical figure need to tell?

- What interests and passions does the historical figure have?

- How could you use language to capture how the individual might recite the poem?

- What poetic devices can you use (e.g., repetition, metaphor, alliteration)?

Questions for Discussion

- What did you learn about the historical figure?

- What are some ways the poems are different? The same?

- What are some examples of words or phrases that reveal where the historical figure is from (places, experiences, people, objects)?

- How did your use of language capture how the historical figure would recite the poem?

Specific Grade Level Ideas

K–2

Students can write "I Am From" poems from the perspective of important historical buildings, statues, and monuments. They can also write "I Am From" poems to explore the ways in which people in a variety of fields have advanced the cause of human rights, equality, and the common good, such as Frederick Douglass, Clara Barton, Elizabeth Blackwell, Jackie Robinson, Rosa Parks, Jonas Salk, and César Chávez. They could also write as though they were major scientists and inventors such as George Washington Carver, Galileo, Marie Curie, Louis Pasteur, or Alexander Graham Bell. Students can write "I Am From" poems from the perspective of sculptures and paintings that reflect the daily life of a culture.

Bio Poems *(cont.)*

3–5

In addition to the K–2 Specific Grade Level Ideas, students can explore the accomplishments of ordinary people in historical situations and how each struggled for individual rights or for the common good, such as James Armistead, Sybil Ludington, Nathan Beman, Lydia Darragh, and Betty Zane. Students could write from the perspective of people who have made significant contributions in the field of transportation, such as Henry Ford, Amelia Earhart, John Glenn, and Sally Ride. Students could also write an "I Am From" poem about economic concepts (e.g., they could write as if they were entrepreneurs who use resources to produce innovative goods and services they hope people will buy). They could also speak from the perspective of places, rivers, cities, and counties to explore the various cultural influences within a particular region.

6–8

Bio poems help students begin to understand how the larger narratives of world history have been represented, the various perspectives and viewpoints, and the importance of bringing marginalized voices to the forefront. Students can write "I Am From" poems to help understand that historical accounts are subject to change based on newly uncovered records and interpretations. Student could explore social and political movements through the eyes of specific individuals.

"I Am From" poems encourage students to use different types of primary and secondary sources and consider the motives, interests, and bias expressed in them. They can use eyewitness accounts, letters, diaries, artifacts, photos, magazine articles, newspaper accounts, and hearsay.

Bio Poems *(cont.)*

9–12

Students can investigate the values of marginalized groups and individuals by writing an "I Am From" poem from the perspective of these groups or individuals. For example, have students write bio poems from the perspective of American Indian tribes that were forcibly removed during Andrew Jackson's presidency, forcing them to embark on the deadly "Trail of Tears" that later prompted American Indian reparation policies. Students can explore the uprooting and maltreatment of American Indian tribes by writing a bio poem from the perspective of Andrew Jackson in order to explore his motivations for ordering the Indian Removal Act of 1830 that resulted in the death of thousands of American Indians (i.e., Jackson's desire to expand U.S. territory for settlers). Students can also write bio poems from the perspective of American Indian chiefs who nobly—yet unsuccessfully—attempted to negotiate treaties and other nonviolent means of resolving the forced migration of American Indians. Have students consider *The Trail of Tears* by Robert Lindneux to analyze how American Indians are represented in the painting and how Lindneux's representation compares to their "I Am From" poems written from the perspective of American Indians.

I Am From History Poem Example, K–5

My Alphabet of Dots
by David Williams

I am from the accident
That stole my sight
And left me in darkness
When I was three.

I am from the city of Coupvray
Where I learned to "read"
What I heard so I could
See the world in my head.

I am from the dreams—
Night after night—
Of a young boy without sight,
Looking
      Looking
            Looking
For a way to read and write
For people who cannot see.

I am from the many,
The countless,
The millions of people
Who now thank me,
200 years later,
For my idea:
An alphabet of dots.

This alphabet is also my name:
Braille.

I Am From History Poem Example, 6–12

I Am From the Darkness

by David Williams

I am from the darkness
That fell upon me
At three.

I am from the accident
That stole my sight
And rendered me thus.

The slip of the awl
On supple leather—
A flash of shining metal
And then the pain.

I am from the Institute
Where the blind were promised books
But denied respect.

I am from the dreams
The haunted sleep
Wherein I sought an answer to the puzzle.

A blind boy
Seeking
  Seeking
    Seeking
A way to encode
The knowledge of the world
In a cypher for the benighted.

I am from the endless years
Of skepticism
And pity
And scorn
And letters that said,
 "No."

"Your dots will not suffice."
"You can never hope to be whole."
"You are, after all, blind."

I am from the beauty of the music
That poured from within me,
The majestic swell of the pipe organ
Filling the gloomy cathedrals of Paris.

I am from the damp
That rose from the Seine
That brought the cough
That doctors called tuberculosis.

The cough
That finally extinguished
The brightest light
The candle in the dark
That showed the way
For all to follow.

I am from
The millions
The countless millions
The sightless millions

Who thank me now
Two hundred years later
Who use my work,
My simple, hard-won triumph:
My alphabet of dots.

And call it by my name:
Braille.

Name _____ Date _____

I Am From History Planner

Directions: Fill in the boxes to brainstorm ideas for an "I Am From" poem. Remember, you are speaking in the voice of your historical figure. Then, on a separate sheet of paper, write your poem, beginning some lines with the phrase "I am from…."

What influenced your historical figure's life?	What turning-point moments took place in your historical figure's life?
What words or quotes did your historical figure actually say?	What is important to know about the time in which your historical figure lived?

Storytelling

Storytelling

Understanding Storytelling

Storytelling has been part of every culture since the beginning of time (Norfolk, Stenson, and Williams 2006). Stories have been used to educate, to inspire, and to entertain. There is the story itself, and then there is the telling of the tale by a skilled teller. Storytellers use language, gesture, eye contact, tone, and inflection as they share a story with an audience. A good storyteller can create a sense of instant community among listeners as well as a deep connection with the material being explored (Hamilton and Weiss 2005). Because the storyteller interacts with the audience as the story is told, listeners often feel that they become part of the story world. They can even feel as if they are co-creators of the story when it is interactive, when connections with characters are developed, and when empathy is established. If you've ever heard a good storyteller tell a compelling story, you know it can transport you to another time and place.

Susan Craig et al. note that "instruction in today's inclusive, culturally and linguistically diverse classrooms requires that teachers understand that there are many different ways of telling a 'good story' besides the traditional, time-sequenced 'school story' format" (2001, 46). In fact, they note that there are varied definitions of what makes a good story in different cultures. Because storytelling involves an interactive connection with the audience, students can change and evolve as stories are told in a less fixed way. This means that students can provide "just the facts," "[stretch] the truth," or "[adjust] the details" to fit the circumstances, depending on how they wish to tell the stories. With this flexible approach, "children co-construct a world view that integrates their mental constructs into the values, struggles, and beliefs of their family and cultural group" (48).

In the following strategies, students benefit from both listening to stories and from becoming storytellers themselves. As listeners, students are supported in their visualization of the stories, which makes a narrative easier to both imagine and remember (Donovan and Pascale 2012). As storytellers, students develop additional skills, including practiced use of voice, improved verbal and nonverbal communication skills, and sense of pacing. Once stories are developed, you can also ask students to write them down, further enhancing their literacy skills.

When your students become storytellers, they fine-tune their communication skills. Oral fluency is developed as students explore vocal tone and inflection, pacing, sound effects, and the addition of rich sensory details to the telling. Listeners feel invited on a journey. Teresa Cherry-Cruz (2001) notes that storytelling supports students in developing "critical speech and language skills to assist children in the evolving process of becoming effective communicators and active listeners who can convey feelings intelligently, succinctly, and convincingly to others across different contextual settings." Also, participating in the creation and telling of stories brings forward students' voices and their ideas.

Storytelling provides vivid contexts that bridge the diverse literacy skills of your students. Students willingly revisit text as they develop, rehearse, tell and retell, and finally write their stories. Craig et al. note that storytelling "provides a social context for literacy, develops oral language skills and the more abstract demands of nonverbal language skills associated with reading and writing literacy, encourages role-taking and inferential comprehension, develops the ability to build a relationship with an audience, as well as taps students' prior knowledge" (2001, 46–47).

Storytelling (cont.)

Strategies for Storytelling

♔ Personification

Some people only use *personification* to refer to assigning human qualities to inanimate objects or ideas and use the term *anthropomorphism* for assigning human qualities to animals. Other folks use these terms interchangeably. We will use *personification* to refer to all such assignment of human characteristics, as it is most familiar to teachers and students, but feel free to use what best fits your curriculum. Personification is an ancient storytelling tool that continues today; think of both Aesop's Fables and the Toy Story movies (Cahill 2006). Stories that give animals and objects human traits allow listeners to think about their shortcomings in a safe way and invite us to think about moral or ethical values. These tales engage learners and allow us to consider different perspectives. Because animals and objects take on human characteristics, the strategy also lends itself to figurative language.

♔ Exaggeration

It's human nature to exaggerate to make our stories more interesting. Often, we hear someone's story and have the desire to top it with something bigger, better, or more grandiose from our own treasure trove of experiences. Storytellers use exaggeration to emphasize their points and to pique the interest of their audiences. In fact, storyteller Jim Green identifies *hyperbole* as a tool in the storyteller's toolbox (Wohlberg 2012). As students create, tell, and retell stories, they are gaining fluency in their communication skills, use of descriptive language, and persuasive abilities.

♔ The Untold Story

In this strategy, students are asked to consider the fact that every story is told from a particular perspective. In foregrounding one vantage point, the viewpoints of others are minimized, marginalized, or even left out. Perspective taking is critical to students' social development, and "understanding perspective of others is an important skill that benefits children in their complex reasoning abilities" (Heagle and Rehfeldt 2006, 32). The Untold Story strategy asks students to consider whose perspective is prominent in a story and what voices or concepts are missing. Inviting students to begin to look for the missing voices or ideas can develop critical-thinking skills and empathy.

Storytelling (cont.)

ᔆ Collaborative Storytelling

Collaborative storytelling often takes place in kids' play (Hourcade, Bederson, and Druin 2003) and has been part of the cultural traditions of many families and communities (Coulter, Michael, and Poynor 2007). Students work together to build a story by adding short segments in their oral telling. Stories can be sparked by graphics, character traits, or settings. The story can be "passed" back and forth, with each teller adding details and information before passing it on. A natural part of the process is a series of unexpected twists and turns that challenge students to maintain a shared story strand, keeping a clear logic so that the story remains together as it unfolds. This challenges them to listen attentively to the details and choices so that they can build on the unfolding events in meaningful and compelling ways by pivoting off details given, such as character traits, circumstances, and actions. Students introduce obstacles and innovative solutions that take the characters on surprising journeys. Jude Yew (2005) notes that constructing knowledge through the collective creation of narratives can provide more effective ways of learning in group settings than learning concepts individually.

ᔆ Retelling

Storytelling is an oral tradition that is grounded in telling and retelling stories. With each retelling, a story grows more polished and more dramatic, with clear high points, striking moments, and building interest and engaging denouements as students experiment with variations in every sharing. Students become more responsive to working with listeners and more adept at using the storytelling process to spark the imagination of the audience. This revisiting of stories also strengthens students' writing skills as stories get honed and more richly detailed with each retelling. Students can use the plot of the story as a flexible frame, improvising as the story unfolds. This builds comprehension skills and also allows students to feel free to adapt the stories based on the responses of listeners, dwelling longer on a particular moment or adding embellishment when needed. This responsiveness heightens awareness of the role of an audience, which translates into students' writing.

Personification

Model Lesson: Geographic Features

Model Lesson Overview

In this lesson, students use personification to tell stories about the geographic features of an area. Through personification, students use the first person perspective of "I" and give voice, human qualities, and point of view to rivers, cities, counties, or other places, telling stories about how they got their names and the cultural influences of a region. In order to inspire ideas, students read a mentor text or listen to a song that personifies a geographic feature.

Standards

K–2

- Knows how areas of a community have changed over time
- Knows the location of school, home, neighborhood, community, state, and country
- Creates or acts out familiar stories, songs, rhymes, and plays in play activities
- Speaks expressively (e.g., uses different voices for various characters)

3–5

- Knows the origin of the names of places, rivers, cities, and counties, and knows the various cultural influences within a particular region
- Knows the approximate location of major continents, mountain ranges, and bodies of water on Earth
- Uses strategies to convey a clear main point when speaking (e.g., expresses ideas in a logical manner, uses specific vocabulary to establish tone and present information)
- Makes basic oral presentations to the class

6–8

- Knows how places and regions serve as cultural symbols
- Knows the ways in which culture influences the perception of places and regions
- Uses level-appropriate vocabulary in speech (e.g., metaphorical language, specialized language, sensory details)
- Makes oral presentations to the class
- Uses appropriate verbal and nonverbal techniques for oral presentations

9–12

- Knows the location of places, geographic features, and patterns of the environment
- Develops, communicates, and sustains characters that communicate with audiences in improvisations and informal or formal productions

Personification (cont.)

Materials

- Mentor texts or songs that personify a geographic feature or place

- Primary and secondary sources about a geographic feature or place

- Craft supplies such as paper, paint, or markers to create props

- *Research Guide* (page 179, researchguide.pdf)

- *Character Development Planner* (page 180, characterplanner.pdf)

- Audio- and/or video-recording software (*optional*)

Preparation

Locate examples of mentor texts or songs that personify a geographic feature or place, such as the song "So Sang the River" by Bill Staines. Plan for students to conduct research on the origins of the names of rivers, cities, counties, or other places and the cultural influences and significance to people and/or animals. Provide students with a text set that includes primary and secondary sources. Decide how you will divide students into small groups. Gather art supplies so that students can create props. Additional ideas are provided in the Specific Grade Level Ideas.

Procedure

1. Activate students' prior knowledge about geographic features or places in the region of study by asking questions such as, "Who do you think named the feature (or place)? What does the name tell us about the culture or time period?"

2. Share the mentor text or song that you chose to demonstrate the personification of a geographic feature or place. Point out how the "character" talks and shows personality, perspective, and voice. Discuss the factual information the character reveals about itself.

3. Assign or allow students to choose a geographic feature or place that they will personify. Distribute the *Research Guide* (page 179) activity sheet and allow time for students to conduct research about their feature or place. Encourage students to browse primary and secondary sources for information as well. Use the Planning Questions to guide students' thinking.

4. Invite students to create and tell the story of their chosen geographic feature or place using the *Character Development Planner* (page 180) activity sheet. Direct students to use it to plan how they will personify their character through voice, movement, descriptive words, and point of view as they tell the story. Provide art supplies for students to create props to use in their storytelling.

Personification (cont.)

5. After students have rehearsed and polished their oral storytelling and feel fluent, have them share their story with the class. Use digital software to record audio and/or video if available. Use the Questions for Discussion to debrief.

6. Have students write down their stories and share their written work with others.

Planning Questions

- What is the origin of the geographic feature or place?

- How can you tell the story of this origin in a compelling way?

- What forces or events influenced the development of the feature or place?

- What has been witnessed over time by the feature or place?

- How will you present the story of this feature or place using the voice of a personified character?

- How will you engage your audience in the story you have to tell?

Questions for Discussion

- What did you learn about the geographic feature or place?

- How did you make the story compelling?

- How did personification help you understand the origin of the name, the cultural influences, and the significance to people or animals?

- Describe the perspective of the character. How did this impact the story?

Specific Grade Level Ideas

K–2

Begin by having students choose an object, a place, or a thing from the classroom and personify it through storytelling. For example, ask them to explore the object's role in the classroom, how and why it got there, and its possible feelings, opinions, wishes, and thoughts. Then, have students focus on the rivers, lakes, landforms, or important buildings in their own community.

Students can also use personification to show why important buildings, statues, and monuments are associated with state and national history. For example, they could tell stories by personifying Mount Rushmore, Angel Island, or the White House.

Personification *(cont.)*

3–5

Students can use personification to tell stories about how physical processes help shape features and patterns on Earth's surface, such as the effects of climate and weather on vegetation, erosion and deposition on landforms, or mudslides on hills. Students can also personify the objects and places associated with important historical figures.

6–8

Students can personify places and regions that serve as cultural symbols, such as the Golden Gate Bridge in San Francisco, California, the Opera House in Sydney, Australia, the Gateway Arch in St. Louis, Missouri, and the Tower Bridge in London, England. They could also personify significant physical features that have influenced historical events: mountain passes that have affected military campaigns, such as the Khyber Pass, Burma Pass, and Brenner Pass; major water crossings that have affected United States history, such as the Tacoma Strait in Washington and the Delaware River near Trenton, NJ; and major water gaps, springs, and other hydrologic features that have affected settlements in the United States, such as the Cumberland Gap, the Ogallala Aquifer, and the artesian wells of the Great Plains.

Students could also personify historical documents and tell the story of how they reflect the values and issues of a time period.

Personification *(cont.)*

9–12

Have students explore significant landmarks and monuments related to the Vietnam War by personifying Maya Lin's Vietnam Veterans Memorial in Washington, DC, that memorializes the U.S. service members who fought in the Vietnam War, those who died in the war, and those who were deemed "missing in action." Have students consider the artistic choices behind the design of the memorial, noting how the design elements of the memorial honor those who died during the Vietnam War. Students can also personify the soldiers represented in the Three Servicemen Statue that is meant to supplement Maya Lin's larger Vietnam Veterans Memorial by using personification to express the thoughts, feelings, emotions, and sentiments of a typical soldier in the Vietnam War. Have students consider the stance of the Three Servicemen Statue as they tell their stories to the class, noting how the stance, weaponry, and military attire communicate messages about the war to onlookers and how this statue works together or against the message conveyed in the Vietnam Veterans Memorial.

Name _____ Date _____

Research Guide

Directions: Use this chart to record information about a geographic feature or place as you research.

Geographic feature or place to be personified:
Origin of name:
How this feature or place came to be:
Cultural influences:
Significance to people or animals:
What has been witnessed over time from the perspective of this feature or place:

Name _____ Date _____

Character Development Planner

Directions: Use this chart to plan how you will personify a geographic feature.

My geographic feature:
Character traits
Voice
Props
Gestures

Exaggeration

Model Lesson: Folk Heroes

Model Lesson Overview

Stories about folk heroes often include exaggeration and provide windows into the culture of the people who told and retold the tales. In this lesson, students read about or listen to a story about a folk hero and identify parts of the story that have been exaggerated. Students then create their own folk hero tale that is set in a historical or present time, and create their own story using exaggeration.

Standards

K–2

- Knows regional folk heroes, stories, or songs that have contributed to the development of the cultural history of the U.S.

- Knows setting, main characters, main events, sequence, narrator, and problems in stories

3–5

- Understands how regional folk heroes and other popular figures have contributed to the cultural history of the United States

- Knows the defining characteristics and structural elements of a variety of literary genres

6–8

- Understands the folklore and other cultural contributions from various regions of the United States and how they helped to form a national heritage

- Understands how descriptions, dialogue, and actions are used to discover, articulate, and justify character motivation

9–12

- Analyzes the values held by specific people who influenced history and the role their values played in influencing history

- Uses a variety of verbal and nonverbal techniques for presentations

Materials

- Background information and artifacts related to folk heroes

- Folk hero mentor texts

- *Exaggeration* (page 185, exaggeration.pdf)

- *Folk Hero Organizer* (page 186, folkhero.pdf)

Exaggeration *(cont.)*

Preparation

Choose a story about a folk hero to tell to students. Practice telling the story aloud, using your voice to make the story even more interesting. Identify exaggerations in the story and decide how to highlight them through gestures and changes in voice. Think about how you can engage students in participating in the story. For example, there may be moments when you invite them to join in by speaking choral lines or by performing gestures to indicate the entrance or action of a character.

Collect background information and artifacts to share with students so that they can better understand the historical and cultural context of the story. For example, if you are telling a story about Daniel Boone, you may want to make copies of United States maps—one from the 1770s and one from 1820—so that students can plot Boone's travels and learn the importance of the pathway he created through Kentucky.

Gather books about folk heroes that students can use as mentor texts to develop their own stories. Additional ideas are provided in the Specific Grade Level Ideas.

Procedure

1. Share with students the background information and historical context of the folk hero tale you will tell. Then, tell the story of the folk hero you have practiced.

2. Retell the story, asking students to hold their thumbs up or make a sound effect that adds to the story as soon as they hear an exaggeration. For example, in a story about Daniel Boone, students could growl like a bear every time they hear an exaggeration.

3. Distribute the *Exaggeration* (page 185) activity sheet to students. Retell the story again, and have students record examples of exaggerations as you go along. Review the truths and exaggerations together as a class.

4. Have students create their own folk heroes and stories. Distribute the *Folk Hero Organizer* (page 186) activity sheet and have students use it along with folk hero mentor texts to plan their stories. Students may work individually, in pairs, or in triads to create their stories. Use the Planning Questions to guide students' thinking.

5. Provide time for students to practice telling their stories. Remind them of the importance of voice and gesture in the development of characters. Ask students to consider how they will portray different characters and how they will move between the roles of narrator and character. How will they match the exaggeration in their stories to their storytelling technique?

Exaggeration *(cont.)*

6. Provide several opportunities for students to tell and retell their stories in small groups. Finally, have students write a version of their stories.

7. Use the Questions for Discussion to debrief.

Planning Questions

- What character traits does your folk hero have? How are these traits relevant to the historical or present time period?

- What problem(s) will your folk hero face?

- How might you use the problem as a way to spark a short story with a beginning, a middle, and an end?

- What will you exaggerate in this story?

- How might you use voice and gesture to emphasize the exaggerations in your story?

- Will part of your story be told by a narrator?

- When might your character speak? How will your voice change to indicate a new speaker?

- How will you add details to invite the audience in?

Questions for Discussion

- How did the storyteller build a story with exaggerations?

- What exaggerations did you identify in the stories?

- What specific words, tones, or gestures helped you create a mental image?

- Why would people prefer to believe exaggerated facts about a folk hero?

- How does this character or story relate to the historical or present times?

- What other famous people in history have benefitted from exaggerated facts about themselves?

Exaggeration (cont.)

Specific Grade Level Ideas

K–2

Introduce the concept of exaggeration by asking students to imagine they are very, very, *very* hungry. Ask them to complete the sentence *I am so hungry I could...* and continue to build to a short story rich with details. Repeat this exercise with *tired* and *excited*. After listening to the story, students can identify the exaggerations they hear without having to record them.

Students can then retell the story you originally told at the beginning of the lesson before creating their own stories. Have them list a sequence of three events that happen in the story. Students can consult this list as they retell it.

3–5

Provide students with a choice of folk heroes from your social studies curriculum. For example, if students are studying the Revolutionary War, consider George Washington, Molly Pitcher, or Paul Revere.

6–8

Encourage students to read several resources related to the folk hero they chose, noting the variety of facts in historical resources as well as in tales. Also, have groups choose heroes from different historical periods or geographical locations to emphasize the relationships among time, place, and tale.

9–12

Have students identify likely folk heroes from contemporary culture, perhaps assigning students to a particular aspect of our culture. For example, if technology is chosen, what tales might they create about Bill Gates, Steve Jobs, or Mark Zuckerberg?

Name _____ Date _____

Exaggeration

Directions: List examples of exaggerated statements in the story. Then, explain why you think the storyteller exaggerated the fact or idea.

Exaggeration	Why do you think the storyteller exaggerated this fact or idea?

Name _____   Date _____

Folk Hero Organizer

Directions: Complete the chart to help you create a story about your folk hero.

My folk hero:	
Historical or present day facts about the time:	Character traits:
Problem my folk hero faced:	What can be exaggerated:
How voice can help exaggerate:	How gestures can help exaggerate:

The Untold Story

Model Lesson: Missing Perspectives

Model Lesson Overview

In this lesson, students listen to or read a story that presents a historical perspective that is minimized, marginalized, or even left out. Students then research multiple perspectives of a time period, consulting primary and secondary sources such as letters, diary entries, digital oral histories, and photographs. Students realize that documentation for untold stories can be hard to find and consider the reasons behind this. Students write an untold story, inventing historical fiction characters and developing their thoughts, feelings, motivations, and experiences. They use critical-thinking skills and develop empathy as they recognize prominent voices and look for the missing voices.

Standards

K–2

- Knows ways in which early explorers and settlers adapted to, used, and changed the environment of the state or region
- Speaks expressively (e.g., uses different voices for various characters)
- Knows setting, main characters, main events, sequence, narrator, and problems in stories

3–5

- Knows who the first explorers of the state or region were
- Knows who the first settlers of the state or region were
- Understands changes that characters undergo
- Understands character point of view

6–8

- Understands that specific individuals and the values those individuals held had an impact on history
- Understands point of view in a literary text
- Understands cause and effect relationships in the development of a plot

9–12

- Analyzes the values held by specific people who influenced history and the role their values played in influencing history
- Conveys individual voice, tone, and point of view in writing

The Untold Story *(cont.)*

Materials

- Nonfiction or historical fiction literature that tells an alternative perspective of a historical event

- Primary and secondary sources about marginalized people, groups, or perspectives

- Video-recording software (*optional*)

- *The Untold Story Plan* (page 191, untoldplan.pdf)

- *Sample Storytelling Techniques* (page 192, storytellingtech.pdf)

Preparation

Choose a book or other text type that presents an untold story of the time period appropriate for your grade level, such as *Jefferson's Sons* by Kimberly Brubaker Bradley or *Encounter* by Jane Yolen. Consider using primary and secondary sources such as interviews, letters, journal entries, or poetry available from the Library of Congress or PBS websites. Plan for students to conduct research on the multiple perspectives of the historical event you are studying. Decide if students will tell their untold story individually, in pairs, or in small groups. It will be important to allow students multiple opportunities to tell their stories aloud before writing them. Consider using digital software to record the oral tellings. Additional ideas are provided in the Specific Grade Level Ideas.

Procedure

1. Activate students' prior knowledge by asking them to think of a familiar story that you have read as a class. Ask students, "From whose perspective is the story told? What perspectives are left out?" Explain to students that it is important to learn about a historical event through the perspectives of all of the people and groups involved.

2. Show students the book or other text type you have selected. Tell students that this text tells an untold story and that it focuses on a perspective that is often left out. Share the text with students and discuss the perspective presented.

3. As a class or in small groups, have students research the multiple perspectives of the historical event you are studying. Have students use library resources and primary and secondary sources of information to explore the various perspectives.

4. Tell students to use the facts they found in their research to imagine and tell an untold story. Distribute *The Untold Story Plan* (page 191) activity sheet to students for use in planning their stories. Use the Planning Questions to guide students in creating their stories.

The Untold Story *(cont.)*

5. Have students practice telling their stories with fluency and expression and then share their stories with the class. Distribute the *Sample Storytelling Techniques* (page 192) activity sheet to students to provide them with effective techniques for telling their stories. If desired, record students telling their stories using available video-recording software. Then, have students write their untold stories.

6. Debrief using the Questions for Discussion.

Planning Questions

- What are the prominent or well-known perspectives of the historical event?

- Who is invisible in the well-known version of the story?

- What untold story will you tell? Why?

- Who are the characters and what are their thoughts, feelings, and motivations?

Questions for Discussion

- What facts from your research did you include? Why?

- What did you learn about this historical event that you did not know before?

- Was it challenging to find historical documents or information about the missing or marginalized perspectives? If so, why do you think this was the case?

- How does the untold story compare to the prominent perspective?

- What did you learn from listening to your peers' untold stories?

- Why is it important to consider an event from multiple perspectives?

The Untold Story *(cont.)*

Specific Grade Level Ideas

K–2

As a class, students can explore the untold stories involved in the journeys of Marco Polo and Christopher Columbus and what happened as a result of their travels. Have students use digital storytelling to tell the story by using web resources such as http://www.littlebirdtales.com.

3–5

Students can research the perspectives involved in the interactions between native peoples and explorers and settlers in a state or region. After providing several opportunities to tell their stories orally in small groups, have students write from the point of view of their character (diary entry, letter, poem, etc.). Consider having students add a visual and/or audio component and tell the untold story, using digital media.

6–8

In addition to the 3–5 Specific Grade Level Ideas, students can read a book such as *The Journal of Wong Ming-Chung: A Chinese Miner* by Laurence Yep to gain a broader perspective of the untold stories associated with the gold rush period. Students could also read texts by Karen Hesse such as *Out of the Dust* that presents childhood voices of the Dust Bowl and the Great Depression. When learning about the civil rights movement, students could also read *Lions of Little Rock* by Kristin Levine and explore the perspectives of those in the town of Little Rock who were silenced but found their voices to stand up for integration. They could also explore the Chicano Movement that happened at the same time as the civil rights movement.

9–12

Students can explore issues in current events such as the untold stories of the animals at factory farms and animal-testing laboratories or the layers of the earth that are being subjected to hydraulic fracturing for natural gas, which is known as *fracking*.

Name _____ Date _____

The Untold Story Plan

Directions: Record details that will help you tell an untold story from a historical time period.

Events:	Characters' feelings:
Setting:	Characters' thoughts:
Historical facts to include:	Characters:

Sample Storytelling Techniques

Find ways to engage the audience. Invite the audience into the story by posing a question.

Repeat lines to heighten audience awareness and add dramatic interest.

Allow your voice to hold emotion, reflecting the intensity of what is happening in the story as it unfolds.

Use facial expressions and eye contact to allow the audience to feel as though they are connected to the story.

Alter the tempo of your speech. Slowing down and speeding up language can intensify the story as the audience is brought along with the pace.

Use descriptive details to help the audience picture the story as it is being told.

Collaborative Storytelling

Model Lesson: Imagining the Past

Model Lesson Overview

In this lesson, students work together to apply their prior knowledge of a historical time period to imagine and tell a story. Using a primary source photograph, a quotation, a diary, a time-period-clothing image, an artifact, or another item, students infer *who*, *what*, *when*, *where*, and *why*, and tell a story by adding short segments to the group's oral telling. The story is "passed" back and forth with each teller adding historical details and information before passing it on. Once the oral storytelling is complete, students research the source that sparked the story and compare facts with fiction.

Standards

K–2

- Knows the differences between toys and games children played long ago and the toys and games of today

- Understands the main idea or message in visual media

- Speaks expressively (e.g., uses different voices for different characters)

- Knows setting, main characters, main events, sequence, narrator, and problems in stories

- Follows conversation rules

3–5

- Understands various aspects of family life, structures, and roles in different cultures and in many eras

- Understands elements of character development in literary works

- Understands the importance of characters' actions to the plot and theme

- Makes basic oral presentations to the class

- Listens to classmates and adults

6–8

- Understands the importance to individuals and society of such economic rights as the right to acquire, use, transfer, and dispose of property; choose one's work and change employment; join labor unions and professional associations; establish and operate a business; copyright and patent; and enter into lawful contracts

- Identifies and analyzes the elements of setting, characterization, plot, and the resolution of the conflict of a story or play

- Makes oral presentations to the class

- Uses strategies to enhance listening comprehension

Collaborative Storytelling *(cont.)*

Materials

- *Primary Source 1* (page 198, primarysource1.pdf)

- *Primary Source 2* (page 199, primarysource2.pdf)

- *Primary Source 3* (page 200, primarysource3.pdf)

- *Collaborative Storytelling Reflection* (page 201, collaborativereflection.pdf)

Preparation

Locate a primary source photograph, quotation, diary entry, sketch, time-period-clothing image, artifact, or other item to use as you model the collaborative storytelling process for students. There are many resources available on the Library of Congress and PBS websites. Primary sources should be from the same event or time period of study as relevant to your grade level and curriculum. Additional ideas are provided in the Specific Grade Level Ideas.

Procedure

1. Activate students' prior knowledge by asking questions about the time period or historical event that they have been studying in the weeks prior to this lesson.

2. Have students form a circle around the room. Explain to them that they will tell a story about the time period or historical event by looking at a primary source and working together collaboratively to tell a compelling story. Tell them that you will model how to begin the story and that you will pass the telling on to the next person. Explain that when the next person gets the story, he or she will add more details or facts and pass it on to the next person in the circle. Remind students that a good story has central characters and events that advance the plot in a way that makes sense.

3. Display the primary source you selected to model for the collaborative storytelling process. If looking at a primary source that portrays politicians with opposing points of view, for example, begin with a compelling lead such as, "Once upon a time, there were two politicians who never seemed to agree…." Turn to the student next to you and invite him or her to continue. When the story has made its way around the circle, ask students what did and did not work and how they could make the story better if they were to revisit it.

4. Divide students into small groups, and, depending on which primary source is appropriate for students and the curriculum, distribute *Primary Source 1* (page 198), *Primary Source 2* (page 199), or *Primary Source 3* (page 200), and have groups analyze the historical significance of the primary source to the time period of study, looking for information that would spark a compelling story.

Collaborative Storytelling *(cont.)*

5. Have student groups work from their knowledge about the time period of study or event and begin to orally tell a story about or inspired by the primary source, including the story elements of *characters*, *setting*, *problem*, *solution*, and *theme*. Tell students that they can tell their story in any manner they find most effective— they do not have to take turns in a circle, but every student must participate. Use the Planning Questions to help students plan their collaborative stories.

6. Have student groups orally tell their story to other groups.

7. Distribute the *Collaborative Storytelling Reflection* (page 201) activity sheet to students and have them research facts about the historical context of the primary source and compare their story to actual details of the time period.

8. Allow time for students to tell their stories to the class. Then, have students individually write the collaborative story, keeping in mind important facts.

9. Discuss the process with students, using the Questions for Discussion.

Planning Questions

- What are the main elements of a story?

- What is the setting of your story?

- Who are the characters? How would each character tell his or her part of the story?

- What is the problem in the story, and how will it be solved?

- What are the moments of action and main transitions in the story?

- How will you make sure the story stays on track by returning to characters introduced and staying with story themes?

Questions for Discussion

- Describe your story's characters, problems, solutions, settings, and themes.

- What were the turning points in the stories?

- How did each character approach the storytelling when it was his or her turn?

- What character traits did you detect based on how each character told the story?

- What was your experience in working collaboratively to tell a story?

- How did your story change after telling it a few different times?

- As you listened to or told stories, what made the storytelling compelling?

- How did your story compare to the actual event?

Collaborative Storytelling (cont.)

Specific Grade Level Ideas

K–2

Students can create collaborative stories about children playing with toys and games from both long ago and today. Student storytellers can weave a tale of what play was like in another time period, painting a picture of that time with rich details and a compelling story that has a clear beginning, middle, and end. The audience can then compare the similarities and differences between long ago and today. For example, the character's feelings and motivations might be the same in addition to ideas about working together and getting along. Create a list of strong verbs and vocabulary words as they arise in the collaborative stories. Invite students to write down their stories. Have students read their stories and record them using available technology. Discuss how the stories change with each retelling.

3–5

Students can use collaborative storytelling to explore concepts about family life at various times throughout history and in different countries and cultures, such as medieval European cities or towns in early America. Invite small groups to create collaborative stories with characters emerging from an illustration, a painting, an artifact, or another primary source. As the story is told from the perspective of a character or narrator, encourage students to work in dramatic moments and conclude with a clear ending that has vivid descriptions as the action progresses. Invite students to write their stories down and add additional scenes, change the ending, or invent new characters.

Collaborative Storytelling *(cont.)*

6–8

Students can tell collaborative stories about the different perspectives depicted in various political cartoons related to labor unions and the debates surrounding workers' rights.

Students can also tell collaborative stories about the process of compromise and the establishment of the Articles of Confederation by exploring the debates surrounding states' rights, issues related to land ordinances, and other responsibilities and opposing views. They can also tell collaborative stories about the lives and accomplishments of select figures from the Renaissance to the Reformation. Have students work together to rewrite the character descriptions, thoughts, and motivations in order to communicate different messages to the listeners. Change the number of storytellers in each group and invite each of them to take on the role of a narrator's voice.

Primary Source 1

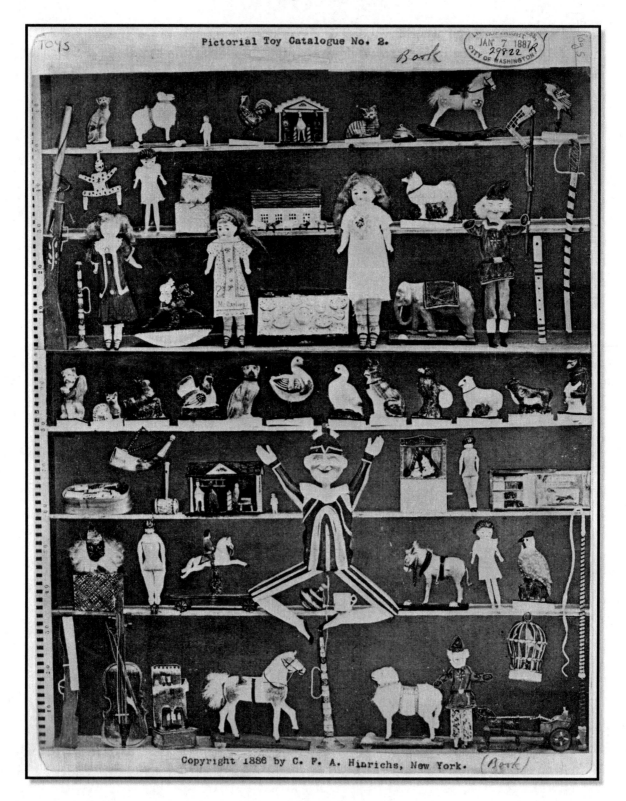

Primary Source 2

Primary Source 3

Name _____ Date _____

Collaborative Storytelling Reflection

Directions: Answer the questions to compare your story with the historically accurate details of the time period from which your primary source originated.

1. Describe the primary source that sparked your collaborative story.

    _____

    _____

    _____

2. Summarize the collaborative story you and your group told.

    _____

    _____

    _____

    _____

3. Research the actual event or time. What really happened?

    _____

    _____

    _____

    _____

4. How do the story and the actual event or time compare?

    _____

    _____

    _____

    _____

Retelling

Model Lesson: Oral Histories

Model Lesson Overview

In this lesson, students learn about the significance of oral histories and listen to audio, watch video clips, or read the transcripts of oral histories. They retell the story of someone from another time and determine the most important aspects of the story. Then, they retell the important parts of the story, adding their own interpretation, language, and props.

Standards

K-2

- Understands cultural heritage through stories
- Understands family heritage through stories
- Uses different voice level, phrasing, and intonation for different situations

3-5

- Knows that families long ago expressed and transmitted their beliefs and values through oral tradition
- Understands that language reflects different regions and cultures
- Uses a variety of verbal communication skills
- Uses a variety of nonverbal communication skills

6-8

- Knows different types of primary and secondary sources and the motives, interests, and bias expressed in them (e.g., eyewitness accounts, letters, diaries, artifacts, photos; magazine articles, newspaper accounts, hearsay)
- Understands that historical accounts are subject to change based on newly uncovered records and interpretations
- Uses a clear point of view in oral presentations
- Uses appropriate verbal and nonverbal techniques for oral presentations

Materials

- Examples of oral histories (audio, video clips, transcripts, etc.)
- *Retelling Plan* (page 205, retellingplan.pdf)

Retelling *(cont.)*

Preparation

Locate examples of oral histories that are relevant and appropriate for your grade level and curriculum. The PBS, Edutopia, and Library of Congress websites are good sources. Additional ideas are provided in the Specific Grade Level Ideas.

Procedure

1. Discuss the concept of oral histories and share the examples of oral histories you found. Ask students to share stories that they pass along and retell over and over in their own families.

2. Model completing the *Retelling Plan* (page 205) activity sheet for students using a sample oral history.

3. Tell students that they will retell the essence of a real oral history. Divide students into small groups and have each group choose an audio, video, or transcript of an oral history.

4. Distribute the *Retelling Plan* activity sheet to students. Have students work together to listen to, watch, or read their group's chosen oral history and complete the *Retelling Plan* activity sheet.

5. Allow students time to practice their retelling, using their *Retelling Plan* activity sheet. Circulate and monitor groups, reminding students that it is all right to leave out some details. Explain that in this type of storytelling, the story is not fixed but shifts with each retelling. They should capture the essence of the story and use their own interpretation. Use the Planning Questions to guide students.

6. Have groups practice retelling with other small groups. Then, invite students to share their stories with the whole class. Have students also write out their retellings, identifying important historical facts and moments.

7. Debrief, using the Questions for Discussion.

Planning Questions

- How will you choose the important moments to retell?

- How will you decide which details to leave out? Why?

- Think about your own life and the stories you have retold. What happens as you retell them?

Retelling (cont.)

Questions for Discussion

- What happened to your story as you retold it again and again?

- What changed? What remained the same?

- How did retelling your story several times affect your ability and confidence as a storyteller?

- What did the retelling of this oral history reveal about the culture, beliefs, values, and experiences of the person telling the story?

Specific Grade Level Ideas

K–2

Invite guest speakers to the classroom who offer different perspectives on one topic. For example, you could invite people with different jobs in the community. Have students create interview questions. As a class, organize their responses into an oral history. Have students retell the stories from different perspectives.

3–5

Students can use retelling to explore environmental issues and ideas about the ways in which the physical environment is stressed by human activities, such as air pollution and water pollution or a current-events issue related to energy use. For example, you could invite guest speakers to the classroom who offer different perspectives on an issue such as erecting windmills in a community. Have students investigate the views of the legislature, health experts, scientists, private companies, and citizens who live near the new windmills. Have students create interview questions and record the interviews. Then, they can organize the sound bites into an oral history.

6–8

Students studying the labor movement in the late 19th century can compare those perspectives to today's labor issues by interviewing different people involved, such as a member of the labor union, a member of management, and everyday workers. Students could also create oral histories to retell stories of those with connections to wars and other historical events. Students can choose an event in recent history, interview different people who experienced the event, and organize the everyday memories into an oral history.

Name _____ Date _____

Retelling Plan

Directions: Work with your small group to discuss and answer the following questions.

1. What are the important parts of the oral history that we need to include in the retelling?

   _____

   _____

   _____

2. What parts or details will we leave out?

   _____

   _____

   _____

3. What details are worth developing further in our retelling?

   _____

   _____

   _____

4. From what point of view will we tell the story (character, narrator, first person, third person, etc.)?

   _____

5. How will we introduce our story?

   _____

   _____

6. How will we interact with the audience (choral moments, gestures for characters, sounds that relate to the story, such as wind blowing)?

   _____

   _____

#51092—*Strategies to Integrate the Arts in Social Studies* © *Shell Education*

Visual Arts

#51092—Strategies to Integrate the Arts in Social Studies

Visual Arts

Understanding Visual Arts

The importance of images and visual media in contemporary culture is changing what it means to be literate in the 21st century. Today's society is highly visual, and visual imagery is no longer supplemental to other forms of information. New digital technologies have made it possible for almost anyone to create and share visual media. Yet the pervasiveness of images and visual media does not necessarily mean that individuals are able to critically view, use, and produce visual content. Individuals must develop these essential skills in order to engage capably in a visually-oriented society. Visual literacy empowers individuals to participate fully in a visual culture.

—Association of College & Research Libraries (2011)

We are bombarded with images on a daily basis, and though we have become more skilled at reading the nontextual representation of ideas, our visual-literacy abilities need to develop further. Why then, is education so often text based? Working with images can provide opportunities for students to observe, notice details, and make meaning. Visual work can communicate nuances that words cannot. In this section, we see how students can use visual art as a language that is more unstructured than text.

Particular to visual arts is hands-on work with various materials. Visual artists use their art in many ways—to create visual narratives, observe, explore patterns, represent concepts, and juxtapose ideas using visual communication. Using the elements of art—*line, form, shape, color, texture,* and *pattern*—students can investigate and create visual representations of ideas. They can also create images as a way to tell what they know.

Integrating the visual arts into social studies is a way to help students see and express social studies concepts visually. Also, when students process visual information as well as verbal, they are using different parts of the brain. Allan Paivio suggests that learning can be expanded by the inclusion of visual imagery, allowing students what he termed "dual coding" (quoted in Reed 2010). All curricular areas have visual aspects, so providing students with the opportunity to work with multiple representations of content is easy to incorporate and will allow students new ways to engage in and access ideas related to social studies.

Visual Arts (cont.)

Strategies for Visual Arts

❧ Visual Narrative

In this strategy, students create and arrange images in sequence to tell a story or create a narrative. The story can be told through images alone, or the pictures can interact with text. Students' understanding of curricular content is enhanced as they create visual narratives that demonstrate or apply their learning. Often, creating a visual narrative makes it easier for students to grasp connections and clarify their thinking, which they can then translate into text. Students can illustrate history concepts, translating their understanding into visual form. Through the visual arts, students can create imagery that represents patterns and visually captures cycles of change and growth that occurred over time.

Visual narratives can culminate in the creation of simple books, digital image essays, magazines, storyboards, comics, and other formats that are easy to make and allow students to compose content and apply and articulate their knowledge in new ways. Teaching artist and researcher Wendy Strauch-Nelson notes that students "seemed drawn to the complementary relationship between the linear style of words and the layered nature of images" (2011, 9).

❧ Representation

Students investigate the ability of the visual arts to communicate information and ideas in compelling ways in order to direct our attention and to add layers of meaning. When students represent social studies concepts through visual art, they translate their understanding into new forms, taking ownership of ideas and engaging with symbolism and metaphor.

David McCandless (2010) notes that we are overwhelmed by information and what he calls "data glut." He suggests that we work with representing data in new ways that prompt us to use our eyes. In this strategy, students create visual work, such as visual essays or infographics, to depict information. Translating historical facts into visual form through this strategy can help students learn about history in fresh and meaningful ways. For example, students may look at how the culture of a civilization has been represented through the Paleolithic cave paintings found in Spain and France by first examining pictographs and applying their observations to create pictographs that represent important messages about classroom procedures.

Visual Arts *(cont.)*

✎ Observation

"Images come before words" (Berger 1972, 7), and looking is one of the first and most pervasive ways we experience the world. A key component of visual art is learning to look closely at the world around us. This can range from noticing and making meaning to sketching and drawing from observation, which requires close attention to detail. Visual images can also provide opportunities for students to observe, attend to details, and make meaning. As cited by Hilary Landorf (2006), Housen and Yenawine found that close observation and discussion of works of art "measurably increases observation skills, evidential reasoning, and speculative abilities, and the ability to find multiple solutions to complex problems" (29). Through this strategy, students recognize the natural fit between history, geography, architecture, and the visual arts.

✎ Mixed Media

This strategy allows students to experiment with putting a range of materials together in new ways. Students manipulate materials, experiment with the juxtaposition of materials, and create two- or three-dimensional pieces such as mobiles, assemblages, dioramas, and digital installations. This process allows students to use metaphors, prompting them to make meaning of experiences in new ways and boil down concepts to their essence to consider qualities rather than literal representations. Students test and explore ideas in experiential, hands-on ways; make choices about how they will use materials to communicate; and explore cause-and-effect relationships in the process of working with different media. The use of multiple representations is essential to the development of flexibly thinking about social studies concepts. This interpretive exploration will draw out other themes. The construction of three-dimensional pieces requires students to interpret and explore ideas visually.

✎ Visual Experimentation

Experimentation is one of the key building blocks of visual art. Artists work with multiple ideas and materials with an element of free play that allows them to investigate and discover ways in which materials can interact with one another. In her research on arts organizations, Shirley Brice-Heath (1999) discusses the language used by artists and students as they talk about "What if?," "How about?," and "Could we try this?" types of questioning. It is through experimenting with materials to see "what if" that imaginative solutions to artistic problems can be developed. The manipulation and experimentation of various materials helps students see how historical concepts relate or interact with one another at a given time or throughout history. Art invites students to apply that knowledge gleaned from experimentation in a playful manner as they create works that use historical understanding in interesting and unusual ways.

Visual Narrative

Model Lesson: Primary Source Digital Story

Model Lesson Overview

In this strategy, students use primary source images and student-created artwork to create digital stories about a historical or present-day event. These visual narratives investigate sequential events, decisions, and cause-and-effect relationships of significant historical events or periods and allow students to share their understanding and insights.

Standards

K–2

- Knows how to identify the beginning, middle, and end of historical stories, myths, and narratives

- Uses technology to publish work appropriate to grades K–2

- Selects prospective ideas for works of art

3–5

- Knows how to identify patterns of change and continuity in the history of the community, state, and nation, and in the lives of people of various cultures from times long ago until today

- Uses technology to publish work appropriate to grades 3–5

- Selects prospective ideas for works of art

6–8

- Understands patterns of change and continuity in the historical succession of related events

- Uses technology to publish work appropriate to grades 6–8

- Understands how symbols, images, sound, and other conventions are used in visual media

9–12

- Understands historical continuity in the historical succession of related events

- Uses technology to publish work appropriate to grades 9–12

- Applies various subjects, symbols, and ideas in one's artworks

Visual Narrative *(cont.)*

Materials

- Examples of visual narratives, such as storyboards or Ken Burns's digital stories

- Primary source photographs that depict aspects of a historical moment

- Software for digital storytelling such as iMovie®, Microsoft Movie Maker®, or Microsoft® Photo Story

- *Storyboard Planner* (page 217, storyboardplanner.pdf)

- Art supplies such as markers, crayons, paint, and pencils

Preparation

Locate examples of Ken Burns's work that turn historical photographs into movies, such as *The Civil War* or *The Statue of Liberty*. Short video clips of Burns's work are often available on the PBS website (http://www.pbs.org/kenburns). Be sure to share a visual narrative that is appropriate for your students by previewing the video clips prior to sharing them with students. Additional suggestions are provided in the Specific Grade Level Ideas.

Procedure

1. Share primary source photographs from the selected time period with students, such as documentary photographer Dorothea Lange's photographs of life in the Depression era. Ask students to identify what the images communicate about the period. Tell students that they will be creating a visual narrative to document life during a specific time period.

2. Explain that a visual narrative is a story told in a sequence of images that are often accompanied by narration. Share examples of Ken Burns's digital stories and discuss how historical events are brought to life through primary source images and artwork. Ask students to notice if there are words and sounds or if the images are shown in silence.

3. Tell students that they will determine how they will break up their historical narratives into meaningful sections. Ask questions such as, "What is the most important information? What sequence makes sense? What images can you add or create to capture the events in terms of sequence and ideas?"

4. Have students locate primary source images and create their own images to tell the sequence of a historical or present day event.

Visual Narrative *(cont.)*

5. Ask students to consider what historical information is provided with the photographs and what is missing. Have students conduct research as needed. Use the Planning Questions to guide students' thinking.

6. Distribute art supplies and the *Storyboard Planner* (page 217) activity sheet to students and have them plan their visual narratives.

7. Have students review their storyboards to evaluate what the visual narrative communicates about the historical time period.

8. Allow time for students to use the chosen software for digital storytelling to create their digital stories. Provide assistance as needed.

9. Provide time for students to share their work with one another.

10. Use the Questions for Discussion to debrief the experience.

Planning Questions

- How will you break up your narrative into meaningful parts?

- What images might you create to help you communicate ideas about this time period?

- Which important moments from the time period will you depict?

- How can you use your storyboard to show action and ideas over time?

- What visual ideas will be important to include?

- How can you arrange the photographs in a meaningful order?

Questions for Discussion

- What did you learn about digital storytelling from creating your storyboard?

- As you read and viewed the work of others, what did you realize about visual narratives?

- What aspects of the time period did your images depict?

- What did you learn about the time period by creating your visual narrative?

- How does a visual narrative communicate differently from a text-based description?

- What other information can be gleaned by looking at the images?

Visual Narrative *(cont.)*

Specific Grade Level Ideas

K–2

Create a visual narrative as a class by having students work together to select images of a time period in their community over time, or students can select images of present day activities such as a student election in order to show democratic values.

Students can explore historical events through visual narrative by investigating concepts related to traditions and cultural celebrations in different societies, past and present family and gender roles, or even investigate hunter-gatherer, agrarian, and pastoral communities.

3–5

Students can use visual narrative to tell the story of important historical discoveries or inventions such as Benjamin Franklin's role in the discovery of electricity and his decisions leading up to it. They could also use visual narrative to construct visual time lines by adding text to indicate the years, decades, or centuries.

Students can also explore through visual narrative the sequence of famous historical events related to famous civil rights leaders, such as Martin Luther King, Jr., Rosa Parks, César Chávez, and Susan B. Anthony, and their respective civil rights causes (e.g., racial equality, workers' rights, gender equality). Students can focus their visual narratives on the various influences of civil rights leaders that made them into strong leaders, or they can focus on the changes that they brought about and the choices and decisions involved in bringing about significant change.

6–8

Invite students to explore historical time periods through digital storytelling such as the Industrial Revolution or the Civil War. Students can also use this strategy to create movie trailers to recommend biographical books to others. Have students research the time period and browse the Library of Congress's website for primary source images.

Students can explore historical events through visual narrative by comparing and contrasting various social systems and their development over time, such as feudalism, monarchies, and city-states in Europe.

Visual Narrative (cont.)

9–12

In addition to the 6–8 Specific Grade Level Ideas, have students use more sophisticated features of the digital storytelling software. They can use webcams to film introductions to the visual narrative, or they can film short discussions about the process that they used to create the digital storyboards.

Encourage students to investigate the democratic process of passing a bill into law through visual narrative by sequencing the steps involved in approving new legislation. Students can focus on the process as a whole or narrow their exploration to a particular step in the approval process to delve into the democratic process in more depth. You can also divide students into groups, having each respective group examine a particular step in depth, and then have students combine their visual narratives to create a class visual narrative about passing new laws.

Name _____ Date _____

Storyboard Planner

Directions: Plan your scenes on this storyboard. Then, write the narration for each scene on a separate sheet of paper.

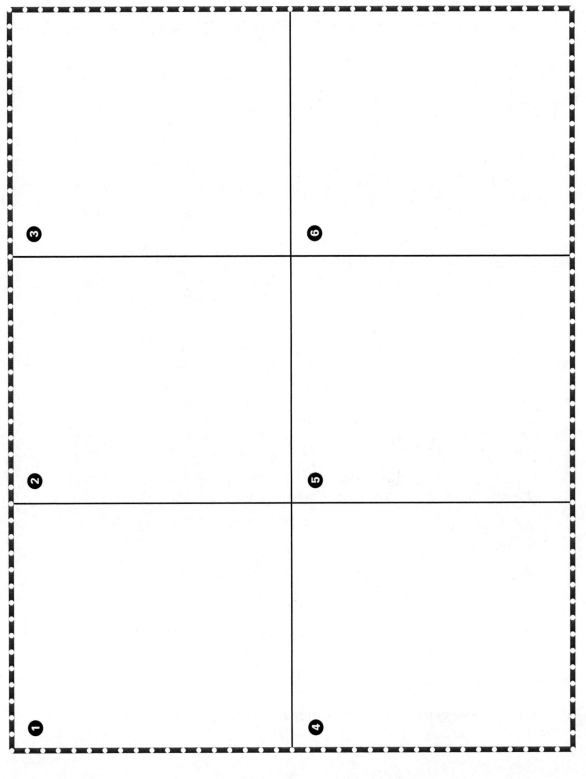

Representation

Model Lesson: An Artistic Reading of World History

Model Lesson Overview

Working with mixed media, students experiment with putting a range of visual arts materials together in new ways to represent their understandings of the possible social and cultural meaning inferred from late Paleolithic cave paintings in Spain and France.

Standards

K–2

- Knows the ways people communicate with each other now and long ago, and the technological developments that facilitated communication
- Knows that people communicated with each other in the past through pictographs
- Knows that art exists from a variety of places and periods of time

3–5

- Understands the origins and changes in methods of writing over time and how the changes made communications between people more effective (e.g., pictographs, cuneiform, hieroglyphics, alphabets)
- Knows that the visual arts are part of the history of various cultures

6–8

- Knows possible social, cultural, and/or religious meanings inferred from late Paleolithic cave paintings found in Spain and France
- Understands how different human communities expressed their beliefs
- Understands how available resources can influence the visual, spatial, or temporal characteristics of a work of art

Materials

- Images of the pictographs on the cave walls in Lascaux, France
- *Pictograph Planner* (page 222, pictoplanner.pdf)
- Art materials such as charcoal, colored pencils, colored chalk, found objects, scrap paper for collage, and watercolor, tempera, or acrylic paints and brushes
- Brown butcher paper

Representation *(cont.)*

Preparation

Locate images of the prehistoric early cave paintings of Lascaux, France (circa 15,000–10,000 BCE Upper Paleolithic) by browsing the Internet or library. If possible, project the paintings on the classroom walls and ceiling at their full size. For more information about the caves and the theories behind early cave art, refer to Salomon Reinach's *Apollo: An Illustrated Manual of the History of Art throughout the Ages* and also Marilyn Stokstad and Michael Cothren's *Art: A Brief History*. Additional ideas are provided in the Specific Grade Level Ideas.

Procedure

1. Ask students, "What are some of the ways we communicate on a daily basis without words?" Record responses for students to reference throughout the lesson. Ask students if they know what *pictographs* are. Explain that they are a very early form of communication in which simple drawings work together to convey meaning.

2. Show students images of the pictographs found on the walls and ceilings of caves in Lascaux, France. If possible, project the pictographs on the classroom walls and ceiling at full size so students have the experience of seeing the vastness of this type of work. Point out parts of the cave paintings where there are painted figures with animal heads and drawings of objects. Ask students to note where the artists used the bulging rocks as part of the animal bodies painted on the wall and ceiling of the cave.

3. Ask students to try to interpret the meaning of each image and how each image contributes to the whole. Ask, "What do you think these pictographs are trying to tell us? Do you think it is a story? What is the story?"

4. Explain to students that these prehistoric artists created paint out of pigments they found and that they developed their own process for applying paint with handmade tools. Tell students that just like the prehistoric artists, they will be using a variety of media to express stories and ideas. Explain that *mixed media* means using a variety of art materials in a single work of art.

5. Tell students they will work in groups to create pictographs that represent an important message about a classroom procedure (e.g., how to proceed safely out of the classroom during a fire drill or how to effectively use each important section of the classroom, such as the reading area or computer area). As a class, brainstorm a list of important classroom procedures to investigate. Record and display students' ideas about important procedures to depict in their artwork.

Representation *(cont.)*

6. Divide students into groups. Have each group choose a procedure they would like to convey. Explain that each group will create a portion of the "cave wall" that will be assembled later. Distribute the *Pictograph Planner* (page 222) activity sheet to students.

7. Distribute a large sheet of brown butcher paper to each group. Direct each group to use charcoal or dark ink to make the outlines of humans, animals, or objects clear and readable. Direct students to also choose two or three different mediums, including found objects, in addition to charcoal or dark ink to use in their paintings. Provide time for students to create their "cave paintings."

8. Once dry, students should crumple their butcher paper so that it takes on a rocky wall effect. Assemble all the sections of the cave wall and hang them to create one large display.

9. View the completed cave wall as a class and use the Questions for Discussion to debrief.

Questions for Discussion

- What purpose do you think the pictographs in the Lascaux caves served?

- What purpose do our pictographs serve?

- What directions do you see depicted on our cave wall?

- How did using mixed media help you convey and represent your message?

Representation *(cont.)*

Specific Grade Level Ideas

K–2

Students can experiment with a variety of materials such as yarn, glue, clay, chalks, charcoals, and pastels in a variety of natural or Earth tones. Discuss with students the special status of images of animals in a variety of cultures. Students could create their own animal with special magical powers that they admire or would like to possess.

3–5

While studying how different early human communities expressed their beliefs through pictographs, students could experiment with making inks from natural resources such as beets or ground coffee and also make their own brushes from found objects like twigs and sticks tied to frayed ropes. Students could also experiment with creating their own alphabet.

6–8

Students can create a mixed-media self-portrait, using collaged magazine images, glue, and paint. Without labeling it with their names, students can tape their self-portrait under a desk or table. Turn the lights off and have students tour all of their neighbors' cave paintings beneath the desks and tables with flashlights. Students can try to identify the artist and the message of the artist's self-portrait.

Name _____ Date _____

Pictograph Planner

Directions: Use the chart to help you plan your pictograph.

Message to be communicated	Ideas and preliminary sketches for pictograph

Observation

Model Lesson: Artist-Observation Field Journals

Model Lesson Overview

Observation has a strong relationship with looking closely at historic artifacts within the context of their environment. This involves the collection of visual data and the act of recording details, information, historic context, and subsequent stories. In this strategy, students create artist field journals and use them as creative observation and research tools in which they document their observations, comparing colonial-period buildings to local historic buildings.

Standards

K–2

- Understands the daily life of a colonial community

- Understands how available resources can influence the visual, spatial, or temporal characteristics of a work of art

3–5

- Understands the historical development and daily life of a colonial community

- Understands how the climate of a place can influence the visual, spatial, or temporal characteristics of a work of art

6–8

- Understands the environmental influences on economic growth

- Understands characteristics of works of art in various art forms that share a similar historical context

- Understands materials and methods unique to specific time periods in the arts

Materials

- Primary source map of the original 13 colonies

- Primary source images that illustrate early colonial architecture

- Resources about architecture in the local community

- Notebooks or handmade field journals

- Colored pencils

- *Architecture Observation Record* (page 227, architecturerecord.pdf)

- Watercolors (basic color palette, tempera paints) and paintbrushes

Observation *(cont.)*

Preparation

Locate a primary source map that shows the original 13 colonies and images that detail early colonial architecture by conducting an Internet search. The Library of Congress website will likely yield good results. Locate photographs and other documentation of a historic building from a different era in your school's area.

If possible, arrange local field trips to view a colonial-period building and another historic building from a different era. If field trips are not possible, gather books and online resources such as photographs and drawings of sites, or conduct an Internet search for virtual tours of historic colonial villages. Additional ideas are provided in the Specific Grade Level Ideas.

Procedure

1. Ask students, "What do we know about the circumstances of people who left Great Britain and came to North America to start a new life?" Ask students if they can name locations in Europe from which some of our early settlers came and contributed to what is called the colonial period.

2. Show a photograph, painting, or drawing of early colonial architecture. Explain that settlers constructed their buildings largely from what they remembered about the buildings from home, but they also learned a tremendous amount about building skills from American Indian tribes.

3. Ask students if they can name the oldest standing building in the school's community. Show students resources that describe the history of the buildings in your area. Then, describe to students how basic early building elements were often created from available local trees (wood), local vegetation (thatch roofing), local rock (foundations), local clay (ceramics or adobe), or local pigments (sources of color).

4. Tell students they will be observing both a colonial-period building and a local building from a different era and record their observations. Explain that many historians use field journals to record their observations of places and artifacts. There is a difference between observing and relying upon memory as opposed to physically creating a field journal in which to document observations. Explain to students that creating artistic field journals will help them strengthen their skills of direct observation of historic artifacts and documentation so they can analyze and interpret what they see.

Observation (cont.)

5. Provide students with notebooks or with folded, stapled drawing paper to serve as field-observation journals in which they record their research. Explain to students that these journals should be used to record their observations, findings, and sketches of colonial buildings and should also include their notes and reflections about what they observe. Provide students with art supplies such as colored pencils, erasers, and watercolors with which to document and illustrate their observations.

6. Have students observe a colonial-period building through a field trip, a virtual field trip, or an examination of photographs or other documentation. Distribute the *Architecture Observation Record* (page 227) activity sheet to students to guide them with their observations. Direct students to make sketches and notes about what they observe, paying particular attention to how available materials from the area were used and how they influenced the building designs.

7. Have students observe a local historical building from a different period through a field trip, a virtual field trip, or an examination of photographs or other documentation, using the same process as in their observation of a colonial-period building. If possible, visit the building so students can make observational drawings, take notes, and do rubbings of textures and watercolor paintings of the local geology, native plants, and other elements present at the site.

8. Using the information collected in their field journals, have students work in small groups to create visual displays showing the similarities and differences between the buildings they observed and how locally available materials influenced the architecture and design. These displays could take the form of posters, storyboards, digital slide shows, or digital mixed-media presentations.

9. Have students present their displays to the class. Use the Questions for Discussion to debrief.

Questions for Discussion

- Using field journals, what did you discover about what life was like for early colonial-period colonists in New England?

- In what way did creating sketches change what you noticed?

- What historical details are present in your images?

- How did settlers use available resources to create buildings?

- What differences did you discover between the colonial building and the local historic building you observed?

Observation *(cont.)*

Specific Grade Level Ideas

K–2

Students can make observations in an artist field journal by examining family artifacts and cultural objects and recording their research and discoveries about their family beliefs and values.

3–5

As an extension, students can research historical paint colors and record the results of experimenting with color mixing in their artist field journals. Students can also make their own writing tools out of locally found objects from nature and make their own inks from local materials.

6–8

Students can create a more complex version of the artist field journal by showing their research, images, and reflections in a digital slide show.

Name _____   Date _____

Architecture Observation Record

Directions: As you observe architectural details of buildings, create sketches of unique details you want to remember, and make notes about your observations.

Architecture Observed	Sketches (include specific details you want to remember)	The materials used, characteristics of architecture, design details, etc.

Mixed Media

Model Lesson: Life Object Assemblages

Model Lesson Overview

In this strategy, students investigate the life of a historical figure through a set of texts, including biographies, historical fiction, videos, and other texts to represent the essence of his or her life through the careful composition of found objects. As students read, view, and discuss the life of this historical figure, they note details about the time period in which the subject lived, such as clothing or textiles, modes of transportation, music played, and architecture. They gather a range of artifacts and create a sculpture, called an *assemblage*, out of the assembled items.

Standards

K–2

- Understands changes in community life over time

- Knows how different media, techniques, and processes are used to communicate ideas, experiences, and stories

3–5

- Understands that specific individuals had a great impact on history

- Knows how different media, techniques, and processes are used to communicate ideas, experiences, and stories

6–8

- Understands that specific individuals and the values those individuals held had an impact on history

- Knows how the qualities and characteristics of art media, techniques, and processes can be used to enhance communication of experiences and ideas

9–12

- Analyzes the values held by specific people who influenced history and the role their values played in influencing history

- Understands how the communication of ideas relates to the media, techniques, and processes one uses

Materials

- Text set about a historical figure (biographies, historical fiction, primary and secondary sources, film clips, etc.)

- Various found objects that represent the lives of historical figures

- *Collecting Ideas* (page 233, collectingideas.pdf)

Mixed Media *(cont.)*

Preparation

Compile a text set that shares the biography of a figure in history, including biographies such as *Benjamin Franklin: An American Life* by Walter Isaacson or *Who Was Sacagawea?* by Judith Bloom Fradin, to use as a model. Collect found objects that represent aspects of this figure's life to share with students. Decide if you will supply students with materials to create their own assemblage items or if you would like them to use found objects. Conduct an Internet search for images of assemblages created by a range of artists such as Louise Nevelson, Joseph Cornell, Wolf Vostell, and Pablo Picasso to share with students. Additional ideas are provided in the Specific Grade Level Ideas.

Procedure

1. Ask students to remember a time in their own lives when they made a difference. Ask questions such as, "What is the memory you have of the event, and how has the memory changed over time? How did the event make you feel? Why do you think you still remember this event? What makes some life events more memorable than others?"

2. Share a descriptive resource from the text set that retells the life events of a historical figure. Discuss with students the events in the resource that were important in the person's life. Ask students, "What contributions did they make? What challenges did they overcome?"

3. Tell students that they will represent the important parts of a historical figure's life through a type of visual arts called *assemblage*. Share pictures of examples of assemblages you have gathered. Explain to students that assemblage is a form of visual arts in which the artwork is created by putting together found objects to communicate an idea, a concept, or another message. Explain to students that their assemblages will tell a story about the contributions of a historical figure.

4. Have students learn more about a historical figure such as Benjamin Franklin or Sacagawea by mining the resources in the text set you have compiled and then brainstorm what they've learned about the person and what information they would like to highlight as they share ideas about the person's life. Tell students to keep notes about objects that might represent the person's life as they read.

5. Once students have sufficiently perused the text set, discuss with students how they might represent the ideas through the collection of actual artifacts or objects that symbolically represent significant life moments of the historical figure. Ask students to identify and collect a variety of artifacts and found objects that represent themes that emerged from the text set.

Mixed Media *(cont.)*

6. Share some of the artifacts or found objects you collected that represent the historical figure's life. If studying Benjamin Franklin, for example, found objects that relate to Franklin's inventions may include swim fins, bifocals, or a kite and a key that suggest his experiments with electricity. Found objects that relate to his work include images of *Poor Richard's Almanac* or letter-press characters to signify his life as a printer. Found objects that relate to his political contributions include a feather pen, designating that he was one of the signatories of the Declaration of Independence. For any historical figure, however, locate artifacts and found objects that highlight important aspects of that figure's life and the contributions he or she made.

7. Once students have collected a range of found objects and artifacts, distribute the *Collecting Ideas* (page 233) activity sheet. Have students categorize the objects they are using as indicated and write about the big ideas behind these objects. Invite students to include their own categories as they become more apparent from the information in the text set.

8. Students are ready to use the found objects to experiment with creating a two- or three-dimensional assemblage. This can be a sculpture or a composed collection of objects presented in a way that is representative of the ideas being conveyed. Students can also include multimodal and multigenre elements such as photographs, recorded music or speech, videos, newspaper clippings, maps, and sketches.

9. Have students write short artist statements about their assemblages as a whole. Have students consider such questions as, "What meaning does the piece hold for you? What is important to communicate?" Provide time for students to present their work to the class.

10. Debrief using the Questions for Discussion.

Questions for Discussion

- What found objects are included in your assemblage?

- How did you select the objects for the assemblage?

- How do the objects and composition of the piece reflect themes that emerged from the text set?

- What moments were represented—big, life-changing events or small yet significant moments?

- What similarities and differences do you see in the ideas selected?

- What artistic choices were made in each assemblage, including the objects selected, the composition of the piece, and how the assemblage was created to communicate information about the historical figure?

Mixed Media (cont.)

Specific Grade Level Ideas

K–2

Have students work in small groups to create an assemblage of a historical figure. Be sure to send home relevant information about the lesson and activity so that family members can help facilitate the reading process and collection of objects and artifacts.

Students can also use this strategy to compare life now and in the past by collecting artifacts from early life that examine colonial and American Indian leaders.

3–5

Explore the genre of biography by having students select a historical figure who has contributed to society, such as Eli Whitney, the inventor of the cotton gin, or Harriet Tubman, who led many slaves to freedom on the Underground Railroad.

Discuss how life stories can be shared textually through words or visually through art. Have students consider the artistic choices they might include to show the idea of a life over time.

Invite students to write a biography of their own lives and the contributions they have made, and represent their lives through found objects that are composed into an assemblage.

6–8

Have students research different perspectives on a historical figure's life and contributions, drawing from a range of sources that include autobiographical statements and materials written from different vantage points. Ask students to find ways to represent conflicting ideas.

Mixed Media (cont.)

9–12

Students can investigate resources about historical figures that focus on changing ideas about race and slavery by exploring the ideas of the opponents of slavery. Have students discuss these ideas and create assemblages that express the views of the opponents of slavery, highlighting the arguments against slavery during various points in history and/or in various regions around the world.

As an extension, students could also discuss the contributions of slaves who were freed, escaped, or aided in the freeing of slaves, such as Harriet Tubman or Dred Scott. Artifacts could also be collected from the antebellum time period of Sojourner Truth.

Name _____ Date _____

Collecting Ideas

Directions: Collect objects that represent your historical figure. Then, categorize the objects. Feel free to include your own categories in the space provided. Then, describe the big ideas behind each object.

My historical figure: _____

Categories	Object	Big Ideas Behind the Object
Different stages of your subject's life, such as childhood and adulthood		
Feelings, such as times when your subject was surprised, thrilled, or sad.		
Different roles a person has played in your subject's life (artist, mother, friend, etc.)		
Important moments such as turning points, signature moments, and cherished memories		

Visual Experimentation

Model Lesson: Culture Collage

Model Lesson Overview

In this strategy, students create two collages that depict different aspects of present-day society by considering the characteristics of their community (e.g., cultural traditions, community characteristics, or hopes for the future). By experimenting with how the visual presentation of the two collages communicates different messages about society, they understand that the existence of many different cultures creates a rich society. Students collect visual materials, cut out images, and layer photographs, sketches, and text into a coherent collage of cultural, environmental, or political ideas.

Standards

K–2

- Understands changes in community life over time

- Experiments with a variety of color, textures, patterns, and shapes

3–5

- Knows how to view the past in terms of the norms and values of the time

- Knows how various concepts and principles are used in the arts and disciplines outside the arts

6–8

- Analyzes the influence specific ideas and beliefs had on a period of history

- Understands what makes different art techniques effective in communicating various ideas

9–12

- Understands that change and continuity are equally probable and natural

- Knows how to perceive past events with historical empathy

- Understands how the communication of ideas relates to the media, techniques, and processes one uses

Materials

- Magazines, newspaper articles, and headlines with images that depict past and present-day societal values and norms

- Examples of work by collage artists

- *Collage Planner* (page 238, collageplanner.pdf)

- Scissors and glue

Visual Experimentation *(cont.)*

Preparation

Gather a variety of present-day sources such as newspapers, magazines (e.g., *TIME®* *for Kids* or *National Geographic Magazine*) and examples of work by collage artists such as Romare Bearden, who work with cultural themes. Additional ideas are provided in the Specific Grade Level Ideas.

Procedure

1. Explain to students the concept of *collage* and that artists use collage as a way to visually share a variety of ideas and perspectives. Share the examples of work by collage artists that were created to investigate concepts in social studies, such as Romare Bearden's work.

2. Tell students that they will be collecting images that represent today's culture within their community. Explain that they will use these images to create two collages that communicate different ideas about society. As a class, brainstorm ideas of how and where students might identify current ideas of culture that have been communicated through images (communication, transportation, community ideals, how the environment affects society, political events, etc.). Use the Planning Questions to guide students in this process.

3. Develop or present students with a present-day issue around which they can create collages. Then, distribute the newspapers, magazines, or other resources students will use to gather images to use in their collages. Encourage students to consider how the images could be arranged in a collage to communicate different messages about society and culture.

4. After students have collected their images, they can categorize them by identifying themes and ideas to frame their collages. Distribute two *Collage Planner* (page 238) activity sheets to students to guide them as they plan their two collages. These categories will help students organize their ideas. They can review the images and identify big ideas that capture the essence of current themes and trends of life in society today.

5. Once students have clear ideas they wish to communicate in their collages, they can begin arranging and juxtaposing images to form their collages. For the first collage, have students experiment with the arrangement of the images to plan for an overall look before gluing the images in place. They can organize ideas around one or more themes. Ask them to add interest to the collage by considering the relationship between images and how choices of color, line, and shape come together to communicate ideas and how those ideas can be layered in a meaningful way. Tell students that the collage should be visually compelling as well as informative about current culture and society.

Visual Experimentation *(cont.)*

6. Have students then create the second collage, encouraging them to experiment with the visual presentation of the collage so that the second collage communicates a message different from the first. Students should consider how the juxtaposition, arrangement, and layering of images contributes to how observers interpret the message of the collage.

7. Have students share and discuss their collages using the Questions for Discussion.

Planning Questions

- How would you describe present-day society?

- What influences shape our culture?

- How would you describe our community's current values?

- What is accepted? What is expected?

- How does society benefit from the influences of multiple cultures?

Questions for Discussion

- What did you discover about our community and culture by viewing the collages?

- Compare your local community influences to the larger society.

- How do societal norms and expectations shape our lives?

- How did the second collage communicate a different idea about society?

- What artistic choices were made in the development of the collages?

- What characteristics of the collages are most revealing?

- What did the images add to our understanding of culture and society?

Specific Grade Level Ideas

K–2

Brainstorm with students different aspects of culture to explore through collage, such as language, music, clothing, food, and basic traditions. Students can work in small groups to find images that represent one category. These images can form a mural-sized collage on a large sheet of butcher paper.

Visual Experimentation *(cont.)*

3–5

Students could create collages on area maps (or other community-based images) by overlaying the geography or roads with images that provide insight about the cultural characteristics of the community. Students could conduct interviews with relatives or community members about their perspective on the current culture and society, drawing out their hopes for the future. Students can collect images that represent these ideas. Browse your local historical society for images from the past to represent the community from long ago. Have students create three-dimensional collages that incorporate artifacts and texture.

6–8

Students could select an issue in today's society that they feel passionate about. Students can create collages to promote activism around an important cause, taking on a point of view and communicating that perspective through collage to affect change in those who observe the collage.

9–12

Students could create digital collages through computer programs such as Glogster™ and draw from statistical sources, visual information, and news articles to record the characteristics of current culture.

Name _____ Date _____

Collage Planner

Directions: Use the planner to guide you as you select images for your collages.

What are the big ideas and characteristics of society today? (language, music, clothing, food, and basic traditions)	What images might you use?	Why?

References Cited

Andersen, Christopher. 2004. "Learning in 'As-If' Worlds: Cognition in Drama in Education." *Theory into Practice* 43 (4): 281–286.

Association of College & Research Libraries. 2011. "ACRL Visual Literacy Competency Standards for Higher Education." Accessed January 16, 2013. http://www.ala.org /acrl/standards/visualliteracy.

Bellisario, Kerrie, and Lisa Donovan with Monica Prendergast. 2012. "Voices from the Field: Teachers' Views on the Relevance of Arts Integration." Unpublished manuscript. Cambridge, MA: Lesley University.

Berger, John. 1972. *Ways of Seeing.* New York: Penguin.

Brice-Heath, Shirley with Adelma Roach. 1999. "Imaginative Actuality: Learning in the Arts During Nonschool Hours." In *Champions of Change: The Impact of the Arts on Learning*, edited by Edward B. Fiske. Washington, DC: Presidents' Committee on the Arts and the Humanities.

Brouillette, Liane, and Lynne Jennings. 2010. "Helping Children Cross Cultural Boundaries in the Borderlands: Arts Integration at Freese Elementary Creates Cultural Bridges." *Journal for Learning through the Arts* 6 (1). http://www.escholarship .org/uc/item/1kf6p9th.

Burnaford, Gail, with Sally Brown, James Doherty, and H. James McLaughlin. 2007. *Arts Integration, Frameworks, Research and Practice.* Washington, DC: Arts Education Partnership.

Cahill, Bryon. 2006. "Ready, Set, Write!" *Writing* 29 (1): 12–15.

Cappiello, Mary Ann, and Erika Thulin Dawes. 2013. *Teaching with Text Sets.* Huntington Beach, CA: Shell Education.

Carpenter, Siri. 2010. "Body of Thought: How Trivial Sensations Can Influence Reasoning, Social Judgment, and Perception." *Scientific American Mind* (January 2011) 38–45.

Center for Applied Special Technology, The. Accessed October 10, 2012. http://www.cast .org/about/index.html.

Cherry-Cruz, Teresa. 2001. "Enhancing Literacy Through the Techniques of Storytelling." *The ASHA Leader.* Accessed January 16, 2013. http://www.asha.org /Publications/leader/2001/011226/storytelling.htm.

Collins, Anne M. 2012a. *50 Leveled Math Problems Level 5.* Huntington Beach, CA: Shell Education.

——. 2012b. *50 Leveled Math Problems Level 6.* Huntington Beach, CA: Shell Education.

Collins, Anne, and Linda Dacey. 2012. *Zeroing in on Number and Operations* series. Portland, ME: Stenhouse.

References Cited (cont.)

Collins, Polly. 2008. "Using Poetry throughout the Curriculum." *Kappa Delta Pi Record* 44 (2): 81–84.

Coulter, Cathy, Charles Michael, and Leslie Poynor. 2007. "Storytelling as Pedagogy: An Unexpected Outcome of Narrative Inquiry." *Curriculum Inquiry* 37 (2): 103–122.

Craig, Susan, Karla Hull, Ann G. Haggart, and Elaine Crowder. 2001. "Storytelling: Addressing the Literacy Needs of Diverse Learners." *TEACHING Exceptional Children* 33 (5): 46-51.

Cremin, Teresa, Kathy Goouch, Louise Blakemore, Emma Goff, and Roger Macdonald. 2006. "Connecting Drama and Writing: Seizing the Moment to Write." *Research in Drama Education* 11 (3): 273–291.

Dacey, Linda. 2012a. *50 Leveled Math Problems Level 1*. Huntington Beach, CA: Shell Education.

———. 2012b. *50 Leveled Math Problems Level 2*. Huntington Beach, CA: Shell Education.

———. 2012c. *50 Leveled Math Problems Level 3*. Huntington Beach, CA: Shell Education.

———. 2012d. *50 Leveled Math Problems Level 4*. Huntington Beach, CA: Shell Education.

Deasy, Richard J. 2002. *Critical Links: Learning in the Arts and Student Academic and Social Development.* Washington, DC: Arts Education Partnership.

Diaz, Gene, Lisa Donovan, and Louise Pascale. 2006. "Integrated Teaching through the Arts." Presentation given at the UNESCO World Conference on Arts Education in Lisbon, Portugal, March 8.

Donovan, Lisa, and Louise Pascale. 2012. *Integrating the Arts Across the Content Areas.* Huntington Beach, CA: Shell Education.

Dunn, Sonja. 1999. "Just What Is a Chant?" Accessed January 16, 2013. http://www. songsforteaching.com/sonjadunn/whatisachant.htm.

Elliott-Johns, Susan E., David Booth, Jennifer Rowsell, Enrique Puig, and Jane Paterson. 2012. "Using Student Voices to Guide Instruction." *Voices from the Middle* 19 (3): 25–31.

Gardner, Howard. 2011. *Frames of Mind: The Theory Of Multiple Intelligences.* 3rd ed. New York: Basic Books.

Growney, JoAnne. 2009. "What Poetry Is Found in Mathematics? What Possibilities Exist for Its Translation?" *Mathematical Intelligencer* 31 (4): 12–14.

Hamilton, Martha, and Mitch Weiss. 2005. *Children Tell Stories: Teaching and Using Storytelling in the Classroom.* Katonah, NY: Richard C. Owen Publishers.

Harp, Bill. 1988. "When the Principal Asks: 'Why Are Your Kids Singing During Reading Time?'" *The Reading Teacher* 41 (4): 454–456.

References Cited (cont.)

Heagle, Amie I., and Ruth Anne Rehfeldt. 2006. "Teaching Perspective-Taking Skills to Typically Developing Children through Derived Relational Responding." *Journal of Early and Intensive Behavior Intervention* 3 (1): 1–34.

Herman, Corie. 2003. "Teaching the Cinquain: The Quintet Recipe." *Teachers & Writers* 34 (5): 19–21.

Hetland, Lois. 2009. "Nilaja Sun's 'No Child'… : Revealing Teaching and Learning through Theater." *Teaching Artist Journal* 7 (1): 34–39.

Hetland, Lois, Ellen Winner, Shirely Veenema, and Kimberly Sheridan. 2007. *Studio Thinking: The Real Benefits of Visual Arts Education*. New York: Teachers College Press.

Hourcade, Juan Pablo, Benjamin B. Bederson, and Allison Druin. 2003. "Building KidPad: An Application for Children's Collaborative Storytelling." *Software: Practice & Experience* 34 (9): 895–914.

Jensen, Eric P. 2001. *Arts With the Brain in Mind*. Alexandria, VA: Association for Supervision and Curriculum Development.

———. 2008. *Brain-Based Learning: The New Paradigm of Teaching*. 2nd edition. Thousand Oaks, CA: Corwin Press.

Kennedy, Randy. 2006. "Guggenheim Study Suggests Arts Education Benefits Literacy Skills." *The New York Times*, July 27.

Kolb, Gayla R. 1996. "Read with a Beat: Developing Literacy through Music and Song." *The Reading Teacher* 50 (1): 76–77.

Kuta, Katherine. 2003. "And who are you?" *Writing* 25 (5): 30–31.

LaBonty, Jan. 1997. "Poetry in the Classroom: Part I." *The Dragon Lode*. 75 (3): 24–26.

Landorf, Hilary. 2006. "What's Going on in This Picture? Visual Thinking Strategies and Adult Learning." *New Horizons in Education & Human Resource Development* 20: 28–32.

Lane, Barry. 1992. *After THE END: Teaching and Learning Creative Revision*. Portsmouth, NH: Heinemann.

Lyon, George Ella. 2010. "Where I'm From." Accessed March 2, 2010. http://www.georgeellalyon.com/where.html.

Marzano, Robert J. 2007. *The Art and Science of Teaching: A Comprehensive Framework For Effective Instruction*. Alexandria, VA: ASCD.

McCandless, David. 2010. "David McCandless: The beauty of data visualization." Filmed July 2010, TED video, 18:17. Posted August 2010. http://www.ted.com/talks/david_mccandless_the_beauty_of_data_visualization.html.

References Cited *(cont.)*

McDermott, Gerald. 1997. *Musicians of the Sun*. New York: Simon & Schuster Books for Young Readers.

McKim, Elizabeth, and Judith W. Steinbergh. 1992. *Beyond Words: Writing Poems With Children: A Guide for Parents and Teachers*. Brookline, MA: Talking Stone Press.

Miller, Etta, Bill Vanderhoof, Henry J. Patterson, and Luther B. Clegg. 1989. "Integrating Drama into the Social Studies Class." *The Clearing House: A Journal of Educational Strategies, Issues, and Ideas* 63 (1): 26–28.

National Council for the Social Studies. 1994. *Expectations of Excellence: Curriculum Standards for Social Studies*. Washington, DC: NCSS.

———. 2008. "A Vision of Powerful Teaching and Learning in the Social Studies: Building Social Understanding and Civic Efficacy." Accessed March 6, 2013. http://www.socialstudies.org/positions/powerful.

National Governors Association Center for Best Practices and Council of Chief State School Officers. 2012. *Common Core State Standards Initiative: The Standards*. Retrieved April 19, 2013, from Common Core State Standards Initiative: http://www.corestandards.org.

New, David. 2009. "Listen." National Film Board of Canada video, 6:21. Accessed October 10, 2012. http://www.nfb.ca/film/listen.

Norfolk, Sherry, Jane Stenson, and Diane Williams. 2006. *The Storytelling Classroom*. Westport, CT: Libraries Unlimited.

Paquette, Kelli R., and Sue A. Rieg. 2008. "Using Music to Support the Literacy Development of Young English Language Learners." *Early Childhood Education Journal* 36 (3): 227–232.

Perret, Peter, and Janet Fox. 2006. *A Well-Tempered Mind: Using Music to Help Children Listen and Learn*. New York: Dana Press.

President's Committee on the Arts and the Humanities. 2011. "Reinvesting in Arts Education: Winning America's Future Through Creative Schools." Accessed January 2, 2013. http://www.pcah.gov/sites/default/files/PCAH_Reinvesting_4web_0.pdf.

Reed, Stephen K. 2010. *Cognition: Theories and Application*. 8th ed. Belmont, CA: Wadsworth Cengage Learning.

Reeves, Douglas. 2007. "Academics and the Arts." *Educational Leadership* 64 (5): 80–81.

Rinne, Luke, Emma Gregory, Julia Yarmolinskyay, and Mariale Hardiman. 2011. "Why Arts Integration Improves Long-Term Retention of Content." *Mind, Brain, and Education* 5 (2): 89–96.

Rosler, Brenda. 2008. "Process Drama in One Fifth-Grade Social Studies Class." *Social Studies* 99 (6): 265–272.

References Cited (cont.)

Schmidt, Laurel. 2011. "Putting the Social Back in Social Studies." *Social Studies Review* 50 (1): 45–47.

Skoning, Stacey N. 2008. "Movement in Dance in the Inclusive Classroom." *TEACHING Exceptional Children Plus* 4 (6): Article 2.

Strauch-Nelson, Wendy J. 2011. "Book Learning: The Cognitive Potential of Bookmaking." *Teaching Artist Journal* 9 (1): 5–15.

Theodorakou, Kalliopi, and Yannis Zervas. 2003. "The Effects of the Creative Movement Teaching Method and the Traditional Teaching Method on Elementary School Children's Self-Esteem." *Sport, Education and Society* 8 (1): 91–104.

"Using Primary Sources." The Library of Congress. Accessed April 2, 2013. http://www.loc.gov/teachers/usingprimarysources/.

Walker, Elaine, Carmine Tabone, and Gustave Weltsek. 2011. "When Achievement Data Meet Drama and Arts Integration." *Language Arts* 88 (5): 365–372.

Waters, Sandie H., and Andrew S. Gibbons. 2004. "Design Languages, Notation Systems, and Instructional Technology: A Case Study." *Educational Technology Research & Development* 52 (2): 57–68.

Wohlberg, Meagan. 2012. "'Don't let the facts spoil a good story': Storyteller Jim Green to release album on Yellowknife's Gold Range." *Slave River Journal* 18.

Yew, Jude. 2005. "*Collaborative Narratives: Collaborative Learning in Blogosphere.*" Master's thesis, University of Michigan. DOI: 2027.42/39368.

Zull, James E. 2002. *The Art of Changing the Brain: Enriching Teaching by Exploring the Biology of Learning.* Sterling, VA: Stylus.

Note-Taking Tool for Observational Assessment

Date: _____

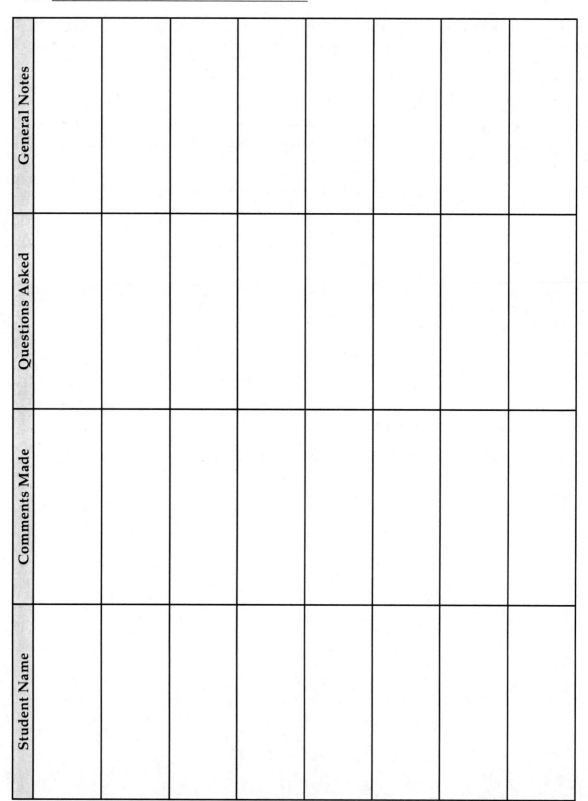

Student Name	Comments Made	Questions Asked	General Notes

Arts Integration Assessment Rubric
for Social Studies

Student Name _____ Date _____

Skill	Beginning	Developing	Meeting	Exceeding
Demonstrates understanding of social studies concepts and skills				
Demonstrates understanding of art concepts and skills				
Communicates thinking clearly				
Demonstrates creative thinking				

Individual Observation Form

Student Name _____ Date _____

Shows understanding (Check all that apply)

_____ Makes representations or notes to understand more fully

_____ Talks with a peer to understand more fully

_____ Asks teacher questions to understand more fully

_____ Helps others to understand

Explains or justifies thinking (Check all that apply)

_____ Communicates thinking clearly

_____ Uses art forms, words, symbols, and writing to summarize thinking
(Underline communication forms that apply)

_____ Uses content vocabulary

Takes it further (Check all that apply)

_____ Makes connections to previous learning

_____ Elaborates on artwork beyond expectations

_____ Suggests new social studies connections

_____ Creates multiple correct responses to task

Printed with the permission of Shell Education (Collins 2012a, 2012b; Dacey 2012a, 2012b, 2012c, 2012d)

Group Observation Form

Student Name _____ Date _____

Use this form to record scores, comments, or both.

Scores: 1—Beginning   2—Developing   3—Meeting   4—Exceeding

Suggests at least one appropriate task solution				
Works cooperatively				
Supports others in their learning				
Communicates clearly, uses correct vocabulary, and builds on the ideas of others				
Provides leadership/ suggestions to group				
Group Members				

Printed with the permission of Shell Education (Collins 2012a, 2012b; Dacey 2012a, 2012b, 2012c, 2012d)

Recommended Resources

Printed Resources

Books

Altman, Linda Jacobs. 1995. *Amelia's Road*. New York: Lee and Low.

Aronson, Marc, and Marina Budhos. 2010. *Sugar Changed the World*. Boston, MA: Clarion. http://sugarchangedtheworld.com/.

Bradley, Kimberly Brubaker. 2011. *Jefferson's Sons*. New York: Dial Books.

Carson, Rachel. 1962. *Silent Spring*. New York: Houghton Mifflin.

Cherry, Lynne. 1990. *The Great Kapok Tree: A Tale of the Amazon Rain Forest*. Boston, MA: Houghton Mifflin Harcourt.

Emerson, Ralph Waldo. 1996. "Concord Hymn." In *The Concord Hymn and Other Poems*. Mineola, NY: Dover Publications.

Fradin, Judith Bloom. 2002. *Who Was Sacagawea?* New York: Grosset & Dunlap.

Hesse, Karen. 1999. *Out of the Dust*. New York: Scholastic.

Hughes, Langston. 1970. "The Negro Speaks of Rivers." In *The Poetry of the Negro 1746–1949*, edited by Langston Hughes and Arna Bontemps. Garden City, NY: Doubleday & Company, Inc.

Isaacson, Walter. 2003. *Benjamin Franklin: An American Life*. New York: Simon & Schuster.

Kalman, Bobbie. 2010. *My Community Long Ago*. New York: Crabtree Publishing.

Kerley, Beverly. 2012. *Those Rebels, John and Tom*. New York: Scholastic.

Komunyakaa, Yusef. 2001. "Facing It." In *Pleasure Dome: New and Collected Poems*. Middletown, CT: Wesleyan University Press.

Levine, Kristin. 2012. *Lions of Little Rock*. New York: Penguin.

Reinach, Salomon. 1907. *Apollo: An Illustrated Manual of the History of Art throughout the Ages*. New York: Charles Scribner's Sons.

Roddy, Ruth Mae. 2000. *Minute Monologues for Kids*. Rancho Mirage, CA: Dramaline.

Stevens, Chambers. 2009. *Magnificent Monologues for Kids 2: More Kids' Monologues for Every Occasion!* South Pasadena, CA: Sandcastle.

Stokstad, Marilyn, and Michael Cothren. 2011. *Art: A Brief History*, 5th ed. Upper Saddle River, NJ: Pearson Education.

Recommended Resources (cont.)

Teasdale, Sara. 1996. "Paris in Spring." In *The Collected Poems*. Cutchogue, NY: Buccaneer Books.

Yep, Laurence. 2000. *The Journal of Wong Ming-Chung: A Chinese Miner.* New York: Scholastic.

Yolen, Jane. 1996. *Encounter.* San Anselmo, CA: Sandpiper.

Periodicals

National Geographic
   http://www.nationalgeographic.com/

TIME® for Kids
   http://www.timeforkids.com/

Audio/Visual Resources

The School of Athens by Raphael
   http://alumni.columbia.edu/multimedia/raphaels-fresco-school-athens

Staines, Bill. 2008. "So Sang the River." YouTube video, 4:00. Posted by "dshorock" on May 20, 2008. http://www.youtube.com/watch?v=eOG8Xx4WfUk.

The Trail of Tears by Robert Lindneux
   http://www.pbs.org/wgbh/aia/part4/4h1567.html

Internet Resources

Edutopia
   http://www.edutopia.org

Library of Congress
   http://www.loc.gov

Little Bird Tales
   http://www.littlebirdtales.com/

The Poetry Foundation
   http://www.poetryfoundation.org/

Public Broadcasting Service (PBS)
   Destination America: http://www.pbs.org/destinationamerica/
   Ken Burns: http://www.pbs.org/kenburns/
   Learning Media: http://www.pbslearningmedia.org/
   Songs of Slavery: http://www.pbs.org/wgbh/amex/singers/sfeature/songs.html
   Woody Guthrie: http://www.pbs.org/wnet/americanmasters/episodes/woody
      -guthrie/aint-got-no-home/623

Recommended Resources *(cont.)*

Note: The following list has been curated from the resource list in *Teaching with Text Sets* by Mary Ann Cappiello and Erica Thulin Dawes (2013, Shell Education, Huntington Beach), used with permission of the authors.

Ancient History

Europe

Multimodal Interactive Overview of Ancient Civilizations, British Museum, London
http://www.ancientcivilizations.co.uk/home_set.html

Multimodal Young Explorers, British Museum, London
http://www.britishmuseum.org/explore/young_explorers1.aspx

NOVA: Ancient Worlds Multimedia Site, Public Broadcasting Service (PBS)
http://www.pbs.org/wgbh/nova/ancient/

Greece

Ancient Greece, British Broadcasting Company (BBC), London
http://www.bbc.co.uk/history/ancient/greeks/

Ancient Greece, Rome, Metropolitan Museum of Art, New York City
http://www.metmuseum.org/toah/ht/?period=04&region=eusb

The Greeks: Crucible of Civilization, Public Broadcasting System (PBS)
http://www.pbs.org/empires/thegreeks/htmlver/

Odysseus Project, Hellenic Ministry of Culture
http://odysseus.culture.gr/index_en.html

Rome

Ancient Rome, British Museum, London
http://www.britishmuseum.org/explore/cultures/europe/ancient_rome.aspx

NOVA: Watering Ancient Rome, Public Broadcasting Service (PBS)
http://www.pbs.org/wgbh/nova/ancient/roman-aqueducts.html

Pompeii, Harcourt Publishers
http://www.harcourtschool.com/activity/pompeii/

The Roman Empire in the First Century, Public Broadcasting System (PBS)
http://www.pbs.org/empires/romans/

Recommended Resources (cont.)

Asia

Asia for Educators, Columbia University
http://afe.easia.columbia.edu/tps/4000bce.htm

Mesopotamia/Iraq

Iraq's Ancient Past, Penn Museum, Philadelphia
http://www.penn.museum/sites/iraq/

Mesopotamia, The British Museum, London
http://www.mesopotamia.co.uk/

Multimodal Tour of Iraq's Ancient Sites, *The New York Times*
http://atwar.blogs.nytimes.com/2011/01/02/a-tour-of-iraqs-ancient-sites/

China

The British Museum, London
http://www.ancientchina.co.uk/menu.html

Freer/Sackler Museum of Asian Art, Smithsonian Museum, Washington, D.C.
http://www.asia.si.edu/collections/chinese.asp

Periods and Dynasties in Ancient China, Metropolitan Museum of Art, New York
Neolithic: http://www.metmuseum.org/toah/hd/cneo/hd_cneo.htm
Bronze (Shang & Zhou): http://www.metmuseum.org/toah/hd/shzh/hd_shzh.htm
Qin: http://www.metmuseum.org/toah/hd/qind/hd_qind.htm

Secrets of the Dead: Terracotta Warriors, Public Broadcasting Service (PBS)
http://www.pbs.org/wnet/secrets/episodes/chinas-terracotta-warriors-watch-the
-full-episode/844/

India

Ancient India, The British Museum, London
http://www.ancientindia.co.uk/

Ancient India, British Broadcasting Company (BBC), London
http://www.bbc.co.uk/history/ancient/india/

Chhatrapati Shivaji Maharaj Vastu Sangrahalaya
http://themuseummumbai.com/home.aspx

The Government Museum of Art and History, Chandigarh, India
http://chdmuseum.nic.in/

South Asian Art, Metropolitan Museum of Art, New York
http://www.metmuseum.org/toah/hd/sasa/hd_sasa.htm

Recommended Resources (cont.)

Japan

National Museum of Japanese History
　　http://www.rekihaku.ac.jp/english/index.html

Periods in Ancient Japan, Metropolitan Museum of Art, New York
　　Neolithic: http://www.metmuseum.org/toah/ht/?period=02&region=eaj
　　Jomon to Yayoi: http://www.metmuseum.org/toah/ht/?period=04&region=eaj

Africa

Egypt

Ancient Egypt, British Broadcasting Company (BBC), London
　　http://www.bbc.co.uk/history/ancient/egyptians/

Collection of NOVA Digital Resources, Public Broadcasting Service (PBS)
　　http://www.pbs.org/wgbh/nova/search/results/page/1?q=ancient+egypt&x=0&y=0

Egyptian Museum and Papyrus Collection, Berlin
　　http://www.egyptian-museum-berlin.com/index.php

Americas

Art of the Ancient Americas, Los Angeles County Museum, Los Angeles
　　http://www.lacma.org/art/collection/art-ancient-americas

Ancient Americas, The Field Museum, Chicago
　　http://archive.fieldmuseum.org/ancientamericas/

Music in the Ancient Andes, Metropolitan Museum of Art, New York
　　http://www.metmuseum.org/toah/hd/muan/hd_muan.htm

NOVA: America's Bog People, Public Broadcasting Service (PBS)
　　http://www.pbs.org/wgbh/nova/ancient/americas-bog-people.html

Medieval History

Creating French Culture: Treasures from the Bibliothèque Nationale de France,
　　Library of Congress
　　http://www.loc.gov/exhibits/bnf/

Medieval and Renaissance Illuminated Manuscripts, New York Public Library,
　　New York
　　http://digitalgallery.nypl.org/nypldigital/explore/dgexplore.cfm?col_id=173

Recommended Resources (cont.)

Medieval and Renaissance Manuscripts, Morgan Library, New York
http://www.themorgan.org/collections/collectionsMedRen.asp

Medieval Art, Metropolitan Museum of Art, New York
http://www.metmuseum.org/toah/hi/te_index.asp?i=15

Medieval Britain, British Broadcasting Service, London
http://www.bbc.co.uk/history/british/middle_ages/

NOVA: Building the Great Cathedrals, Public Broadcasting Service (PBS)
http://www.pbs.org/wgbh/nova/ancient/building-gothic-cathedrals.html

NOVA: China's Age of Invention, Public Broadcasting Service (PBS)
http://www.pbs.org/wgbh/nova/ancient/song-dynasty.html

NOVA: Medieval Siege, Public Broadcasting Service (PBS)
http://www.pbs.org/wgbh/nova/lostempires/trebuchet/

NOVA: Who Were the Vikings?, Public Broadcasting Service (PBS)
http://www.pbs.org/wgbh/nova/ancient/who-were-vikings.html

Treasures of Islamic Manuscript Paintings, Morgan Library, New York
http://www.themorgan.org/collections/works/islamic/default.asp

Native American History

The American Experience: Native Americans and The Transcontinental Railroad, Public
Broadcasting Service (PBS)
http://www.pbs.org/wgbh/americanexperience/features/interview/tcrr-interview/

The American Experience: We Shall Remain, Public Broadcasting Service (PBS)
http://www.pbs.org/wgbh/amex/weshallremain/

Indian Country Today Media Network
http://indiancountrytodaymedianetwork.com/

Native American Public Telecommunications
http://www.nativetelecom.org/

Native Americans, Library of Congress, Washington
http://www.loc.gov/teachers/classroommaterials/themes/native-americans/

Recommended Resources (cont.)

Colonial American History and the American Revolution

The American Revolution Center, Philadelphia
http://www.americanrevolutioncenter.org/

The American Revolution, The History Channel
http://www.history.com/topics/american-revolution

Ben Franklin, Public Broadcasting Service (PBS)
http://www.pbs.org/benfranklin/

Boston National Historic Park, National Park Service
http://www.nps.gov/bost/index.htm

Colonial and Early America, Library of Congress
http://www.loc.gov/teachers/classroommaterials/themes/colonial-america/

Connecticut Historical Society
http://www.chs.org/

George Washington, Mt. Vernon Historic Site
http://www.mountvernon.org/

Georgia Historical Society
http://www.georgiahistory.com/

Historical Society of Pennsylvania
http://hsp.org/

Images of the American Revolution, Teaching with Documents, The National Archives
http://www.archives.gov/education/lessons/revolution-images/

Liberty! The American Revolution, Public Broadcasting Service (PBS)
http://www.pbs.org/ktca/liberty/

Library of Congress: Jamestown Settlement
http://www.loc.gov/teachers/classroommaterials/primarysourcesets/jamestown/

Maine Historical Society
http://www.mainehistory.org/

Massachusetts Historical Society
http://www.masshist.org/

New York Historical Society Museum and Library
http://www.nyhistory.org/

Patrick Henry, Red Hill Historic Site
http://www.redhill.org/index.html

Recommended Resources (cont.)

Paul Revere House
http://www.paulreverehouse.org/

Preservation Virginia: Jamestown Rediscovery
http://www.apva.org/rediscovery/page.php?page_id=1

Thomas Jefferson, Monticello Historic Site
http://www.monticello.org/

Williamsburg, Virginia
http://www.history.org/

"Within These Walls" Exhibit of Colonial House, 200 Years of History,
American History Museum, Smithsonian
http://americanhistory.si.edu/house/

The Civil War

"1861: A Social History of the Civil War," National Public Radio
http://www.npr.org/2012/03/09/146936196/1861-a-social-history-of-the-civil-war

Abraham Lincoln Papers, Library of Congress
http://memory.loc.gov/ammem/alhtml/malhome.html

Abolition of the Slave Trade, Schomberg Center, New York Public Library
http://abolition.nypl.org/home/

African American Soldiers in the Civil War, The Library of Congress
http://www.loc.gov/teachers/classroommaterials/presentationsandactivities
/presentations/timeline/civilwar/aasoldrs/

American Civil War (1861-1865), *The New York Times*
http://topics.nytimes.com/topics/reference/timestopics/subjects/c/civil_war_us
/index.html

The American Experience: Abraham and Mary Lincoln: A House Divided,
Public Broadcasting Service (PBS)
http://www.pbs.org/wgbh/americanexperience/films/lincolns/

Britain's Abolition, British Broadcasting Company (BBC), London
http://www.bbc.co.uk/history/british/abolition/

The Civil War: 150 Years, National Park Service
http://www.nps.gov/features/waso/cw150th/index.html

Civil War Exhibits of the Smithsonian Institution
http://civilwar150.si.edu/

Recommended Resources (cont.)

Discovering the Civil War, National Archives, Washington, DC
http://www.archives.gov/exhibits/civil-war/

Ford's Theatre, House Where Lincoln Died, National Historic Site
http://www.nps.gov/foth/index.htm

Library of Congress: African-American Odyssey: Free Blacks in the Antebellum Period
http://memory.loc.gov/ammem/aaohtml/exhibit/aopart2.html

Library of Congress: Civil War Music: When Johnny Comes Marching Home
http://www.loc.gov/teachers/classroommaterials/primarysourcesets/civil-war
-music/

National Geographic Underground Railroad Site
http://www.nationalgeographic.com/railroad/

National Underground Railroad Freedom Center
http://www.freedomcenter.org/underground-railroad-0

The New York Historical Society: Slavery in New York
http://www.slaveryinnewyork.org/

Slavery and the Making of America: PBS Online Resources
http://www.pbs.org/wnet/slavery/

Slavery in the North
http://www.slavenorth.com/slavenorth.htm

"Unknown No More: Identifying a Civil War Solider," National Public Radio
http://www.npr.org/2012/04/11/150288978/unknown-no-more-identifying-a-civil
-war-soldier

Women in the Civil War
http://www.history.com/topics/women-in-the-civil-war

Industrialization

The African-American Mosaic, Chicago: Destination for the Great Migration,
Library of Congress
http://www.loc.gov/exhibits/african/afam011.html

"Great Migration: The African-American Exodus North," National Public Radio
http://www.npr.org/templates/story/story.php?storyId=129827444

The Industrial Revolution in the United States, Library of Congress
http://www.loc.gov/teachers/classroommaterials/primarysourcesets/industrial
-revolution/

Recommended Resources (cont.)

Lowell National Historic Site, National Park Service
http://www.nps.gov/lowe/index.htm

Teaching with Documents: Photographs of Lewis Hine: Documentation of Child Labor, National Archives
http://www.archives.gov/education/lessons/hine-photos/

Victorian Britain: Children in Factories, British Broadcasting Service (BBC)
http://www.bbc.co.uk/schools/primaryhistory/victorian_britain/children_in _factories/

World War I

Experiencing War: Stories from the Veterans History Project, World War I, Library of Congress
http://www.loc.gov/vets/stories/ex-war-wwi.html

The Great War and the Shaping of the 20th Century, Public Broadcasting Service (PBS)
http://www.pbs.org/greatwar/

World War I (1914-1918), *The New York Times*
http://topics.nytimes.com/topics/reference/timestopics/subjects/w/world_war_i_/

World War I: Their Stories, British Broadcasting Company (BBC), London
http://www.bbc.co.uk/history/worldwars/wwone/

World War I Web Guide, Library of Congress
http://www.loc.gov/rr/program/bib/wwi/wwi.html

World War II

Children of World War II, British Broadcasting Company (BBC), London
http://www.bbc.co.uk/schools/primaryhistory/world_war2/

Experiencing War: Stories from the Veterans History Project, World War II, Library of Congress
http://www.loc.gov/vets/stories/wwiilist.html

Manzanar National Historic Site, National Park Service
http://www.nps.gov/manz/

Official Site: Navajo Code Talkers, Arizona
http://www.navajocodetalkers.org/

Perilous Fight: America's World War II in Color, Public Broadcasting Service (PBS)
http://www.pbs.org/perilousfight/

Recommended Resources (cont.)

World War II (1939–45), *The New York Times*
   http://topics.nytimes.com/top/reference/timestopics/subjects/w/world_war_ii_/

World War II Aviation, Air and Space Museum, Smithsonian Institute
   http://airandspace.si.edu/exhibitions/gal205/

World War II Records, National Archives
   http://www.archives.gov/research/military/ww2/

World War II Remembered, Scholastic
   http://teacher.scholastic.com/activities/wwii/

World War II Web Guide, Library of Congress
   http://www.loc.gov/rr/program/bib/WW2/WW2bib.html

The Holocaust

Anne Frank House, Amsterdam
   http://www.annefrank.org/

Jewish Museum, Berlin
   http://www.jmberlin.de/main/EN/homepage-EN.php

Museum of Jewish Heritage: A Living Memorial to the Holocaust, New York
   http://www.history.com/topics/the-holocaust

United States Holocaust Memorial Museum, Washington
   http://www.ushmm.org/

Yad Vashem, World Holocaust Center, Jerusalem
   http://www.yadvashem.org/

The Civil Rights Movement

1955–1956: The Story of the Montgomery Bus Boycott, *The Montgomery Advertiser*
   http://www.montgomeryboycott.com/newspaper-front-pages

African American Museum in Philadelphia
   http://aampmuseum.org/

American Experience: Freedom Riders, Public Broadcasting Service (PBS)
   http://www.pbs.org/wgbh/americanexperience/freedomriders/

Birmingham Civil Rights Institute, Birmingham
   http://www.bcri.org/index.html

Recommended Resources (cont.)

Martin Luther King Jr. Historic Site, National Park Service
http://www.nps.gov/malu/index.htm

Separate is Not Equal, Brown vs. Board of Education, National Museum of American
History, Smithsonian Institute
http://americanhistory.si.edu/brown/index.html

Stories of Freedom and Justice, National Museum of American History,
Smithsonian Institute
http://americanhistory.si.edu/freedomandjustice/learning_resources

Contents of the Digital Resource CD

Page Number	Resource Title	Filename
N/A	Correlation to the Standards	standards.pdf
31	Embodiment Brainstorming Guide	embrainstormingguide.pdf embrainstormingguide.doc
32	Observing Others	observingothers.pdf observingothers.doc
37	Moving through Time	throughtime.pdf throughtime.doc
42	Movement Pathways	pathways.pdf
43	Choreography Planner	choreographyplanner.pdf choreographyplanner.doc
49–50	Six Qualities of Movement Reference Sheet	qualitiessheet.pdf
51	Transportation Technology Effects	transporteffects.pdf transporteffects.doc
56	Movement Suggestions	movesuggestions.pdf movesuggestions.doc
57	Differing Perspectives	differing.pdf differing.doc
69	Tableaux Ideas	tableauxideas.pdf tableauxideas.doc
70	Gallery Walk Observation Sheet	gallerywalk.pdf gallerywalk.doc
75	Drama Planner	dramaplanner.pdf dramaplanner.doc
76	Reading Reflection	readingreflection.pdf readingreflection.doc
82	Affecting History	affectinghistory.pdf affectinghistory.doc
83	Sample Monologue: Rachel Carson	monorachelcarson.pdf
84	Monologue Planner	monologueplanner.pdf monologueplanner.doc
89	Getting Ready for Improvisation	improvisation.pdf improvisation.doc
94–95	Script Ideas	scriptideas.pdf scriptideas.doc
96	Observation Record	observationrecord.pdf observationrecord.doc
106	Found Sounds	foundsounds.pdf foundsounds.doc
111	Lyric Brainstorming Guide	lyricbrainstorming.pdf lyricbrainstorming.doc

Contents of the Digital Resource CD (cont.)

Page Number	Resource Title	Filename
112	Songwriting Planner	songwritingplanner.pdf songwritingplanner.doc
113	Famine Song, Grades K–5	famineK–5.pdf
114	Famine Song, Grades 6–12	famine6–12.pdf
N/A	"Famine Song, Grades K–5"	famineK–5.mp3
N/A	"Famine Song, Grades 6–12"	famine6–12.mp3
N/A	"Famine Song" Instrumental Version	famineinstrumental.mp3
118	Sample Chants	chants.pdf
119	Chant Planner	chantplanner.pdf chantplanner.doc
124	Soundscape Planner	soundscapeplanner.pdf soundscapeplanner.doc
129	Meaning of the Lyrics	meaninglyrics.pdf meaninglyrics.doc
130	Mash-Up Planner	mashupplanner.pdf mashupplanner.doc
141	Example Dialogue Poem	dialoguepoem.pdf
142	Two Voices Poem Plan	twovoicesplan.pdf twovoicesplan.doc
147	My Poem About History	poemabouthistory.pdf poemabouthistory.doc
152	Poetry Word List	wordlist.pdf wordlist.doc
157	Cinquain Examples	cinquainexamples.pdf
158	Word-Count Cinquain Planner	cinquainplanner1.pdf cinquainplanner1.doc
159	Parts of Speech Cinquain Planner	cinquainplanner2.pdf cinquainplanner2.doc
160	Syllables Cinquain Planner	cinquainplanner3.pdf cinquainplanner3.doc
166	I Am From History Poem Example, K–5	iamfromK–5.pdf
167	I Am From History Poem Example, 6–12	iamfrom6–12.pdf
168	I Am From History Planner	iamfromplanner.pdf iamfromplanner.doc
179	Research Guide	researchguide.pdf researchguide.doc
180	Character Development Planner	characterplanner.pdf characterplanner.doc

Contents of the Digital Resource CD *(cont.)*

Page Number	Resource Title	Filename
185	Exaggeration	exaggeration.pdf exaggeration.doc
186	Folk Hero Organizer	folkhero.pdf folkhero.doc
191	The Untold Story Plan	untoldplan.pdf untoldplan.doc
192	Sample Storytelling Techniques	storytellingtech.pdf
198	Primary Source 1	primarysource1.pdf
199	Primary Source 2	primarysource2.pdf
200	Primary Source 3	primarysource3.pdf
201	Collaborative Storytelling Reflection	collaborativereflection.pdf collaborativereflection.doc
205	Retelling Plan	retellingplan.pdf retellingplan.doc
217	Storyboard Planner	storyboardplanner.pdf storyboardplanner.doc
222	Pictograph Planner	pictoplanner.pdf pictoplanner.doc
227	Architecture Observation Record	architecturerecord.pdf architecturerecord.doc
233	Collecting Ideas	collectingideas.pdf collectingideas.doc
238	Collage Planner	collageplanner.pdf collageplanner.doc
244	Note-Taking Tool for Observational Assessment	notetaking.pdf
245	Arts Integration Assessment Rubric for Social Studies	assessmentrubric.pdf
246	Individual Observation Form	individualform.pdf
247	Group Observation Form	groupform.pdf